TROUT AND GRAYLING

AN ANGLER'S NATURAL HISTORY

Trout and Grayling
An Angler's Natural History

Norman Maclean
Reader in Biology, Southampton University

ADAM AND CHARLES BLACK
LONDON

First published 1980
A & C Black (Publishers) Limited
35 Bedford Row, London WC1R 4JH

ISBN 0 7136 2044 7

Maclean, Norman, *b. 1932*
Trout and grayling.
1. Grayling 2. Trout
3. Grayling fishing 4. Trout fishing
I. Title
597′·55 QL638.S2

ISBN 0 7136 2044 7

Printed in Great Britain by
Morrison & Gibb Ltd., London and Edinburgh

Contents

List of Illustrations

Figures

Tables

Plates (between pages 84 & 85)

Acknowledgements

Besides the people mentioned in the Preface, many others have contributed to the formation of this book. The author and publisher would like to thank those who have generously provided figures and plates or given permission to use previously published material, among whom are the following:

Figures

1.1 Roy Eaton, *Trout & Salmon.*
2.2 *The Trout*, W. E. Frost & M. E. Brown, Collins 1967.
2.7 *The Vertebrate Eye and its Adaptive Radiation*, G. L. Walls, Carnbrook Press, USA, 1942.
3.1 *British and Irish Salmonidae*, Francis Day, Williams & Norgate 1887.
3.2 *A Study of Fishes*, Chapman Pincher, Herbert Jenkins Limited 1947.
3.3 *The Trout*, W. E. Frost & M. E. Brown, Collins 1967, adapted from *Textbook of Zoology* (Vol II), T. J. Parker & W. A. Haswell, Macmillan 1962.
3.4 *Ørretboka*, I. D. Sømme, Jacob Dybwads Forlag, Oslo 1948.
6.1 Corby (Northants) and District Water Company.
7.1 Dennis Green, Royal Society for the Protection of Birds.
7.2 & 7.3 *The Study of Instinct*, M. Tinbergen, Clarendon Press, 1951.
9.2 *Facts from Figures*, M. J. Moroney, Penguin Books Limited 1957.

Plates

1 *The Complete Freshwater Fishes of the British Isles*, Jonathan Newdick, A & C Black (Publishers) Limited 1979.
2 & 8 Jenny Mallinson & Ken Collins, Southampton University Sub Aqua Club and the Department of Oceanography, Southampton University.
3 *Trout Fly Recognition*, John Goddard, A & C Black (Publishers) Limited 1966.
4 R. N. Campbell, *Journal of Fish Biology* (Vol XIV) 1979, Academic Press Inc (London) Ltd; Copyright: Fisheries Society of the British Isles.
6 Graham Swanson, Stourton, Wiltshire.
7 *Grzimeks Tierleben, Enzyklopädie des Tierreiches* (Vol IV), Kindler Verlag, Zurich, 1968.

Preface

This book arose out of a winter of frustrating weather which inhibited my usual weekend grayling fishing. Instead of fishing, I worked off my frustration by writing and thinking about fishing. But I hope the book may achieve more than relief of my piscatorial enthusiasm. Being a professional biologist (though not, I must stress, a fish biologist) as well as an angler, it seemed to me that I could make some small contribution to the success and enjoyment of my fellow anglers by discussing with them both the fundamental biology of trout and grayling and some of the recent advances in scientific understanding of fish diet and fish behaviour.

The whole complexion of game fishing has radically changed in the last decade, fishing in stocked stillwaters for rainbow trout having largely replaced the earlier emphasis on river fishing for browns. This angling revolution has rendered many standard books on game fishing little more than a nostalgic stirring of old memories. I have tried to make this book relevant to the present situation.

If my professional connections have given me some benefit as an angling writer, that advantage can never outweigh my fortune in my friends. Hampshire enjoys a concentration of fishing assets and professional skills, and three local people have each made a signal contribution to this book, both by sharing with me their knowledge and experience and by critically reading through the entire draft of the book. These three, to whom I record my great appreciation, are Bernard Aldrich, Head Keeper on the Broadlands stretch of the river Test, Alex Behrendt, owner of the Two Lakes Fishery near Romsey, and Dick Houghton, Keeper on the Lower Itchen Fisheries stretch of the river Itchen. I am also greatly indebted to some of my professional colleagues for reading and commenting on certain of the chapters, in particular to Dr John Allen, Dr Clive Bennett, and Dr Stephen Wratten.

Although the generous efforts of these people have certainly reduced the number of errors in the book, some may remain. Much of the fun of fishing is because mysteries persist, and where uncertainty prevails, strong opinions thrive. I must therefore ask the forbearance of my readers if their favourite water is quite unlike anything I have discussed herein.

I have also been lucky in my publishers and the stout efforts and good advice of Leonard Brown and Bridget Chamberlain deserve my best thanks. Many people have helped with typing, especially Anne Ager, to whom I am most grateful for both speed and accuracy.

Southampton 1979.

To the memory of
my father-in-law
Gavin L. Smith
farmer and gentleman

1

Classification and Characteristics of the Fish

We are here concerned with two fish which, although appearing to be very different, are fairly closely related in that they both belong to the same family of fishes, called the *Salmonidae*. Anglers frequently refer to this group as 'game fishes' although many fishermen in Britain seem often to be ignorant or forgetful that the grayling belongs with this group. It is an interesting family of fish for a number of reasons, not the least of which is that zoologists believe them to be amongst the most primitive bony fishes (the cartilaginous fish – sharks, rays and skate, evolved earlier than did the bony fishes: the latter are termed Teleosts in zoological classification). Fossils of early salmon-like fish are to be found in cretaceous rocks, deposited about one hundred million years ago, so the original 'salmonids' did not have to worry about distinguishing between natural and artificial flies! No anglers were around then!

Characteristics of Salmonids

In order to satisfy ourselves about the authentic relationship between trout and grayling as well as to deepen our appreciation of them as fish, we must consider the diagnostic features of salmonids and some of the interesting fishes which are included in this grouping. The characters of most interest to the angler include (1) the presence of scales on the body but absence of scales from the head, (2) the presence of many caecae (blind tubes) attached to the fore part of the intestine (see Chapter 3), (3) eggs which, in the female, are shed directly into the body cavity, (4) absence of barbels (tactile sensory organs on either side of the mouth, as in catfishes, carp etc.) and (5) two dorsal fins, of which the posterior one is reduced to a fatty stump, the so-called 'adipose' fin. In practice the last character is the best known and most obvious.

Trout and grayling therefore enjoy the best of pedigrees, being closely related to the noble salmon and, along with that splendid fish, belonging to the most ancient tribe of boned fishes. Before considering the characteristics of trout and grayling themselves, consideration must be given to other salmonids of particular interest to fishermen. These are the Atlantic salmon, the Pacific chum salmon, the humpback salmon, the smelt, the vendace, the powan, the huchen, and the Arctic char.

As most readers will know, the so-called scientific names of animals and plants consist of two parts, each in Latin and both conventionally printed in italics. The first part is the generic name and indicates the name of the main group to which the organism belongs, and therefore many different animals may share the same generic name. Following the generic name is the specific name and this is unique to the particular species. I will return to the interesting but complex question of what is a species and a subspecies in the context of the varieties of trout later in this chapter.

The ATLANTIC SALMON, *Salmo salar*, is well known to all of us, and I will not discuss it at length here. If only I had more experience of fishing for it, then this book might well have been enlarged to encompass it in detail. Alas, I must admire *Salmo salar* from afar, watching it as a naturalist and biologist but very rarely pursuing it as an angler. It is, of course, a migratory fish, spending much of its life in the sea but returning to fresh water to breed. They are thus said to be andromatous. Atlantic salmon and large sea trout are sometimes difficult to distinguish. Perhaps the most obvious difference between the two fish is the insertion of the tail, which is thick in the trout and more slender in the salmon. This explains why it is common practice to 'tail' salmon by grasping them in one hand just in front of the tail fin. Large trout cannot be reliably handled in this way. Trout tails are also rather straight-ended, that of the salmon slightly more forked.

A more reliable but painstaking distinction between salmon and trout lies in counting the scales between the lateral line and adipose fin. In the trout the number varies between 14 and 19 and is most commonly 16, while in the salmon the number is between 11 and 15 and commonly 12 to 14.

The PACIFIC CHUM SALMON, *Oncorhynchus keta*, is slightly smaller than the Atlantic salmon. It has been introduced to some Russian rivers but to my knowledge has not so far been reported from Europe. Like *Salmon salar* it is andromatous, but tends to be more reddish in colour on entering fresh water and its flesh is less desirable to eat than that of the Atlantic species.

The HUMPBACK SALMON, *Oncorhynchus gorbuscha*, is so called because the male spawning fish is distinctly humpbacked, as well as being of a very dark red colour. Adults of this species invariably die after spawning, as do also the chum salmon, and this explains the astonishing tales of American rivers being almost blocked by the bodies of dead salmon in late autumn. By comparison with an Atlantic salmon, the humpback is a fairly small fish. As with the chum, the humpback has been introduced into the Russian White Sea area and, interestingly for the British angler, it has very occasionally been caught in Scottish and northern English waters, presumably having migrated round the north of Scandinavia.

Various bodies have suggested the introduction of chum and humpback salmon to British rivers, but these have been opposed on the grounds of a supposed threat to existing stocks of the superior Atlantic salmon.

The SMELT, VENDACE and POWAN. These three salmonid species, whose Latin names I will not use to trouble my readers' composure, are of somewhat local and specialised interest. Smelt are partially migratory, spawning in fresh water but living much of the time in brackish estuarine waters. The size of the smelt shoals seem to vary greatly from year to year, and they are commercially exploited for food and oil extraction in a few British localities and more especially along the North European coast and the Baltic. Vendace and powan are interesting to us in that they resemble grayling quite closely, although lacking the striking dorsal fin of the latter species. They, and some other salmonids, are often referred to as whitefishes. Both are European fishes with migratory populations in the Baltic Sea and land-locked populations in many lakes, including lakes in Wales, north-west England and Scotland. Personally, I have not had experience of fishing for any of these three species so I will not discuss them further.

The HUCHEN, *Hucho hucho*, is an outstanding game fish resembling a slender rainbow-lustred Atlantic salmon. Despite its non-migratory habits it regularly grows to a size substantially greater than *Salmo salar* (I say, despite non-migration, since the sea clearly affords a far richer feeding ground than a freshwater river), but its distribution is sadly very restricted, being confined to the Danube and its tributaries and a few lakes in that area. Experimental introduction to other rivers has so far proved unsuccessful and indeed resident stocks in the Danube are reported to be very depleted. Probably only a few British rivers could be expected to support the growth of this splendid fish – I am thinking of rivers such as the Aberdeenshire Don and Hampshire Itchen, both with reputations for supporting good populations of natural trout, and with substantial natural coarse fish populations.

The ARCTIC CHAR, *Salvelinus alpinus*, is a very beautiful fish, somewhat resembling a trout but with strikingly reddish belly and ventral fins. It occurs as a land-locked species in many European lakes, including some in Ireland, Wales, north-west England and Scotland, but rarely exceeds 2lbs in weight in such situations. The best forms of this excellent fish are the migratory populations, common in all rivers draining into the

Arctic seas. I have had splendid sport catching Arctic char in some very cold rivers in Norwegian Lapland, and here, although the run did not last for long, the sport on a downstream wet fly was outstanding. The fish were so abundant that, after a few days, my camping companions allowed me to go fishing only on the understanding that I did not bring back any fish!

GRAYLING AND TROUT, THE SPECIES AND HYBRIDS

Now that we have considered some of their interesting and exciting relatives, let us concentrate on the species with which this book is chiefly concerned, the trout and grayling. Since the grayling is a single species without important hybrids, we will give it first consideration, leaving the bulk of this chapter to a discussion of trout species

The GRAYLING, *Thymallus thymallus*, is a charming and beautiful fish, whose Latin name refers to the thyme-like smell which comes from a freshly caught specimen. Although substantially a river fish, associated with clean fast-flowing streams, it also occurs in lakes in Northern Europe, and indeed there are populations of grayling in a few reservoirs, and there are said to be grayling in more than one English lake – for example Bala Lake in Gwynedd. I should here like to acknowledge a valuable source of information on the biology and distribution of grayling – an M.Sc. Thesis by Chandra Pal Singh at the University of Southampton entitled 'Some Contributions to the Biology of Grayling'. Singh records the presence of grayling in a large number of British rivers, and concludes that it is not a native British fish but has been widely introduced (see *Table 1.1*). He records the introduction of three dozen grayling into the Scottish Clyde in 1939, a river in which they are now abundant. The presence of grayling in the Cumberland Eden is also attributed to stocking of a 'handful of fingerlings' in 1880. The

England

Northumberland: Derwent, Blyth, Till, Glen and Breamish
Durham: Tees, at least between Winston and Croft
Cumberland and Westmorland: Eden and Eamont
Lancashire: Ribble, Hodder
Yorkshire: Ure, Swale, Wharfe, Nidd, Derwent, Rye, Costa, Seren, Dove, Riccal and in Gouthwaite Reservoir
Lincolnshire: Gwash
Derbyshire: Dove, Derwent and Wye, Manifold and Lathbill
Herefordshire: Lugg, Arrow, Teme, Monnow, and a few reported in Frome
Cheshire: Dee, Alwen Lliw, and Llanfor
Shropshire: Severn
Suffolk: Lark
Buckinghamshire: Chess
Cambridge: Ivel (recent introduction)
Gloucester and Somerset: Chew, Frome, Boyd and Bis and occasionally in Bristol Avon
Devon: Exe, between Thorveton and Bolham
Cornwall: Upper Tamar
Hampshire and Wiltshire: Test, Anton, Dever, Dunn, Itchen, Avon, Wylye, Nadder, and lower Bourne

Scotland Clyde, Tay and Tweed

Wales Bala Lake, Dee (upper reaches)

Table 1.1 Distribution of Grayling in Britain

Information based partly on:

Platts W. C. (1936) 'The grayling'. *Salm. Trout. Mag.* No. 82
Singh C. P. (1959) 'Some contribution to the Biology of Grayling' (M.Sc. Thesis, Southampton University)

fact that grayling are very difficult to rear and transport presumably accounts for their continued restriction to only a few river systems. Grayling in Britain rarely grow to the multi-pound class found in many celebrated Central European river systems, although grayling of ten years old are not uncommon in most good grayling rivers. The fish is, I think, absent from Ireland.

Trout species and hybrids

We must now turn to the most interesting but complex part of this chapter: a discussion of that outstanding tribe of game fishes, the trout. Since trout are a variable group, I would ask my patient reader to take a good grip on his chair, a firm bite on his pipe, and give me a little more of his attention than I would normally demand (or perhaps deserve) for there will now follow an attempt to define exactly what a *species* is, and so to explain why, for example, brown and sea trout are regarded as the same species, but the rainbow a separate species.

Here goes. A species is a population of freely interbreeding individuals, isolated from other species by reproductive barriers, and the individuals often, but not always, being closely similar to one another in appearance and behaviour. This definition means that breeding in the wild should be possible between members of the same species. Breeding between individuals of different species may take place in the artificial environment of a zoo, or of course be engineered by artificial fertilisation as in the mixing of eggs and milt of differing fish species. Hybrids resulting from the interbreeding of different species are often but not invariably sterile.

What of the phrase 'reproductive barriers'? This simply implies that there are commonly obstacles to interbreeding between different species, and that such obstacles are normally associated with the actual process of reproduction. Thus neighbouring related species may have different courtship behaviour, or there may be anatomical obstacles to copulation.

My definition concluded with a phrase on similarity in appearance and behaviour. This is the aspect of speciation of which most people are aware, and it should simply be stressed that such similarity is often far from perfect. We know that in our own species no two individuals are exactly alike and that races with differing skin colour exist. So with other organisms, individuals may be of the same species and sex but look markedly different in appearance. The separation of animals and plants into distinct species is itself a result of the process of evolution and we may encounter situations in the wild where a clear distinction cannot be drawn. Scientists talk of 'good species' and 'bad species', meaning ones that are neatly separated, and ones that are not neatly separated. Often within a species two rather distinct populations of individuals may exist, sometimes with a partial breeding barrier. These populations are often referred to as subspecies, and a third Latin name may be used to indicate this. An excellent example is provided by our British bird the carrion crow, found in England and the Scottish lowlands, but entirely replaced in the Highlands and Ireland by the quite distinct subspecies, the hooded crow. The winter- and spring-spawning rainbows are partially isolated in terms of reproduction and so are regarded as subspecies – *Salmo gairdneri irideus* – the migratory steelhead, and *Salmo gairdneri shasta* – the non-migratory autumn-spawning rainbow favoured by British fish farmers.

Now that we have, I trust, successfully traversed the nice problem of speciation, let us turn our attention, with a tinge of satisfaction, to the actual species and subspecies of trout, their relationships and characteristics. The first to be discussed will be three American species of only secondary importance to British anglers. I hope you will forgive me when you discover (as you now will directly when you spot their Latin names) that two of these species are actually char and not trout, that is, their generic name is *Salvelinus* and not *Salmo*. But since they are commonly called trout I have seen best to discuss them here.

AMERICAN LAKE TROUT, *Salvelinus namaycush*. This is a sturdy fish beloved of American anglers. It may grow to a very large size – 17lbs and above. It is olive coloured and heavily though irregularly spotted. Although successfully introduced into certain Swiss lakes, it is not known to have been introduced into British waters.

AMERICAN BROOK TROUT OR SPECKLED TROUT, *Salvelinus fontinalis*. Another char, this fish is very colourful, especially, of course, in the breeding season, and resembles a highly coloured rainbow trout. It is a lover of fast gravelly rivers and mountain brooks, and although it does not attain any great size – 2lb fish are regarded as very large – it is a highly prized sporting fish, especially for fly fishers. Unlike the lake trout, the brook trout has been introduced into a number of British rivers, but although it remains as a breeding fish it has not become widespread.

Of great interest is its ability to hybridise with both rainbow and brown trout. Such hybrids are, of course, intra-generic crosses between a char and a true trout, and they are invariably sterile (some hybrids between closely related species may be fertile, though usually the fertility of all hybrids is low). In passing, it should be said that hybrid animals and plants often display what is called by the geneticist 'heterosis' or 'hybrid vigour'. This simply means that first generation hybrids are often better all-round organisms than either parent, having more of the 'good' of both and less of the 'bad'. (For the purists and scientists amongst us, I can say that heterosis is widely believed to result from increased heterozygosity, but we need hardly discuss that theory here.)

Perhaps it is worth emphasising that hybrid vigour is very much a first generation affair. If such hybrids are fertile and are cross-bred amongst themselves, the offspring would most commonly be inferior both to their parents and to the separate species, their grandparents.

The hybrids between the American brook trout and the brown trout have a striped appearance and are often termed zebra or tiger trout. Such a cross has appeared naturally in Britain in Wise Een Tarn where both parents are found (recorded in Frost and Brown's book, *The Trout*). These tiger trout are also reared artificially on a limited scale and, since they are sterile, have been employed as a strictly temporary introduction to an angling water on an experimental basis. The cross which produces tiger trout is reported to be most easily accomplished by using eggs from brown trout and milt from the char or brook trout. Crosses between brook trout and rainbows are also possible but I have at present no information on their characteristics.

CUT-THROAT TROUT, *Salmo clarki*. This fish is a true trout, deriving its common name from the slash of red which appears on the throat. Like the rainbow, it is native to the western United States and west Canada (the brook trout is an eastern species and the lake trout is found chiefly in Canada in the Great Lakes area). As with the lake trout, this species has been used occasionally in Europe as an introduction, and hybrids between this species and the rainbow have been occasionally reported.

RAINBOW TROUT, *Salmo gairdneri*. We now move into territory very familiar to all game fishermen the world over, the topic of the rainbow trout. The debt owed by anglers to this species can hardly be exaggerated, since it has proved an extremely adaptable fish, both in still and running waters. A detailed description of the rainbow is scarcely necessary, although its immediate distinction from the brown can be noted – a broad iridescent purple line along the flanks, and a spotted tail. Rainbows can grow to a very large size, the world record apparently being held by American fish, where a rod-caught fish of 51lbs is reported (see discussion in *Trout & Salmon* by L. Straight, September 1978) and less official reports of seine-netted specimens of up to 56lbs are known. There have been many reports of British record rainbows between 15 and 20lbs in weight. My own view of some of these records is that they should be differentiated from records of truly wild fish, since fish in lakes which are under close management may well respond dramatically to additional feed provided, especially if such feed contained small amounts of any growth hormone (whether or not it does, I do not know). The Olympic Games may not be the sole sporting venue with problematical legislation about the use of steroid therapy! I have no fixed ideas on what our present or future attitude should be to the use of hormones in fish rearing, except that their use should always be declared, but it certainly provides us with a topic for argument.

While on the subject of the size of the rainbow trout it should also be mentioned that fish rendered artificially sterile – the fishy equivalent of a bullock – may also gain weight more rapidly, and that such sterilisation techniques achieved either hormonally or by irradiation are involved in a few experimental farms in the production of fish for the table.

As was mentioned earlier in this chapter, two subspecies of the rainbow exist, *Shasta* and *Irideus*. *Shasta* is a non-migratory autumn spawner used very widely in fish farming and for introduction to angling waters. It is particularly useful for introduction to river fisheries since, being non-migratory, it is not normally lost to the sea. They are more tolerant of warm and even polluted water than is our native brown trout, but are less rigid in their feeding behaviour. That is, rainbow trout tend to wander more in a river system rather than adopt a fixed territory as does our native brown. Moreover, rainbow occasionally show some slight shoaling tendency in lakes, although this may often be a temporary response following introduction to a new water.

Shasta rainbow have become naturalised breeding fish in a few rivers, for example, the Derbyshire Wye and the Chess in the Chilterns.

Irideus or steelhead rainbow are andromatous, that is, they feed substantially at sea and return to fresh water to breed. Land-locked *irideus* are found in many places, especially such countries as South Africa and New Zealand, and in these conditions they thrive but do not breed. Attempts to introduce steelheads as a breeding population to British rivers have been made but have not proved successful. *Irideus* rainbow spawn late, sometimes not until March, and waters using such fish for stocking should have a late opening date. Very dark out-of-condition rainbows encountered in late April in some stocked fisheries are either *irideus* rainbow or *shasta x irideus* mixed stock. Being the same species, the two populations can be hybridised, but only with some difficulty (and in specialised situations) since the spawning times overlap only slightly. Rainbow trout of both strains, but especially the *shasta* race, mature more quickly and grow more rapidly than brown trout but are shorter-lived. Although the rainbows used as stock fish are commonly described as of '*shasta* type', most are likely to be of mixed heritage with a trace of *irideus* but mainly *shasta* characteristics. Rainbow tend to die naturally when five or six years old while old brown trout may be anything up to twenty years older.

The question is often asked whether rainbows compete with brown trout when both are present in rivers or lakes. The answer seems to be that in lakes quite a lot of straight competition may occur in high population densities but very little competition is apparent in streams and rivers. This no doubt follows from the highly territorial behaviour of the brown and the nomadic habits of the rainbow in river systems. Of course, brown trout do move within their territory, especially between a 'home retreat' situation which may be under a bank or weedbed and used as a refuge, and the chosen feeding situation which is likely to be at the tail of an eddy where flies and nymphs are carried into a bottle-neck of current. We have probably all seen brown trout on the move between lair and normal feeding station, a distance in a river of anything up to twenty yards. The behaviour of the rainbow is often quite different, since a permanent lair is less apparent and while fixed feeding at a productive eddy may occur, feeding in a 'beat' is more common. This demands that the upstream fly fisherman must follow a fish on its way upstream and be careful to hide if it turns to return downstream. Feeding in a fixed perambulation (that really means walking round – is there an equivalent word for swimming round?) is common with both browns and rainbows in lakes, but most evident in the latter fish.

Hybrids between browns and rainbows can be reared following artificial fertilisation of the eggs. Such hybrids are often of a beautiful brown or golden colour but spotted, and are almost invariably sterile. They are not obviously superior to either parent in growth rate or 'sporting' behaviour: in this case, seemingly, hybrid vigour is not very evident.

BROWN TROUT, *Salmo trutta*. The taxonomy and relationships of the brown trout are both intriguing and perplexing. Time was when what we now know as one species was subdivided into many species, for example the river brown trout, then dubbed as *Salmo fario*; the sea trout as *Salmo eriox*; the lake trout *Salmo lacustris*; the large lake trout *Salmo ferox*, and so on. Local names are no less confusing with the 'gillaroo' of some Irish loughs – a beautiful and brightly coloured fish; the 'Loch Leven trout' from the loch of that name, and the myriad of vernacular names for sea trout – herling, truff, whitling, sewin, peal and phinnock. A full discussion of the life of the sea trout can be found in Hall's book, *The Life of the Sea Trout*, published in 1930.

The brown trout is now reliably regarded as a single species, and many of the varied forms as simply responses to specialised environments. Moreover, many scientists would insist that no reliable subspecies exist. However, if you are a 'splitter' in taxonomy you may be permitted to recognise three subspecies; *Salmo trutta fario*, the brown trout of most lakes and rivers; *Salmo fario eriox*, the migratory sea trout; and *Salmo fario lacustris*, a migratory lake trout of some Alpine waters which migrates to breed in rivers which feed the lake, returning to the lake each year after breeding.

Brown trout are readily distinguished from rainbows by the lack of spots on the tail fin, as well as by the frequent but not invariable spots on the body, many of them red. Migratory

Fig. 1.1 Photograph of a splendid 4 lb 'gillaroo', a strain of brown trout found in some Irish loughs. This one was taken from Lough Mask and is held by James Murphy.

sea-going trout become silvered like salmon and it is often difficult to differentiate with certainty between the two species (see discussion on page 21). Sea trout of the British east coast are often distinguished from the sewin of Wales, Ireland and the western seaboard by their longer and larger heads and more massive fins. It should be stressed that many river brown trout may visit the sea or estuarine waters for varied periods of time, and may return to the river silvered but for a few black spots. Although sea and river brown trout are regarded as being the same species, hybrids between the races are themselves distinctive and display some traces of 'hybrid vigour'. This is especially evident in the hardiness of the eggs and fry. If sea trout are pond-reared they mostly resemble normal riverine brown trout in colour but retain a migratory instinct, for at least one generation. A proportion do however become brightly silvered, showing clearly that the adoption of a silver colour is not itself dependent on actually visiting the sea.

Brown trout x salmon hybrids may be reared, most readily by using brown trout milt to fertilise salmon eggs, but the fry are reported to suffer a high mortality. The hybrids resemble trout more than salmon. Interestingly, they are not necessarily sterile, and second generation hybrids have been reared.

This then completes our brief survey of the salmonid family and the relationships between its members. Some aspects of these relationships are dealt with in Chapter 4, where the life histories of trout and grayling and the effects of heredity and environment on their character are discussed in more detail.

2

Some Basic Biology – External

This chapter is not intended to provide an encyclopaedic account of the anatomy of game fishes, but rather some background knowledge about the way our quarry the fish is put together. Much of it is already part of the know-how of any experienced fisherman and it is the sort of knowledge which not only helps, sometimes, to catch more fish, but greatly enhances one's enjoyment of fishing. Just as knowing a little about push-rods and pistons can add a new and satisfying dimension to driving a car, so knowing something about fish anatomy and engineering enhances the pleasure of watching and catching fish.

Let us assume that a fish, trout or grayling, has just been caught and is now safely on the bank. You will already have noticed as you took him from the landing net that, beautiful as he is, he is very slimy. The slime, or mucilage, to give it its proper name, is present in order to reduce friction between fish and water, enabling the fish to swim more easily. It is also partly protective in that it has quite considerable anti-bacterial properties, so reducing infection of the skin by parasites or invading bacteria. As you wipe your hands clean – I'm afraid mine are usually wiped on my trousers! – take a moment to look at the external features of the fish.

Fins and scales

Glance first at the fins (see *Fig. 2.1*). The large tail fin, the caudal fin to the biologist, is the main propeller of the fish, and is firmly embedded in muscle and well attached to the end of the vertebral column or backbone. That is really what we are up against when fighting a trout; we are essentially fighting the

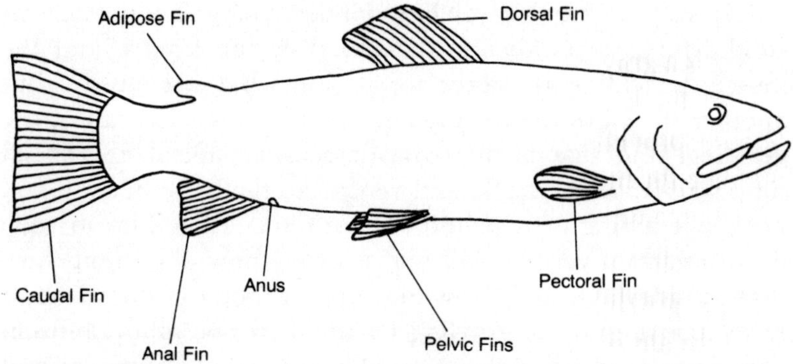

Fig. 2.1 Diagram of a Salmonid fish showing the arrangement of fins.

caudal fin. The fish's ability to flex that caudal muscle drives him through the water, and makes big fish proportionately more difficult to bring to the net. Of course, once the tail has done its work and the fish has gained speed, we are also contending with the problem of stopping weight. We all remember that feeling of being attached to a submarine, usually just before our leader snaps! Healthy big fish have relatively massive tails and plenty of good muscle to work them. It has been calculated that, at speed, a large trout will travel at about 15 knots. It follows that the art of landing large fish from stillwater consists in sustaining the first run, when the fish is virtually unstoppable, and then exerting sideways pressure, but averting further major runs. In rivers, it is also imperative to stay downstream of the fish, so avoiding the combination of tail and current in the fight. Weight for weight, it is quite probable that trout can wield more muscle in the movement of their tails than can salmon. This is because the salmon tail, although massive, is less thick at the base, and permits salmon to be landed by 'tailing', that is gripping with the hand between body and caudal fin. In a trout the insertion of the caudal fin is much thicker, so providing much less of a finger-hold between body and caudal fin.

If it is a grayling that you have landed, you will notice that its caudal fin is certainly less massive than the trout's, and the muscle providing the force for it somewhat less sturdy. But another fin more than compensates for the weaker tail of the grayling, and that is the fantastic sail-like dorsal fin (dorsal simply refers to the back, and ventral to the belly side). If you hook a grayling of a pound or more and allow him to slide downstream of you, he will find a strong flow of current, turn slightly sideways, and erect that huge canopy of dorsal fin. I recall hooking a fine grayling on the Test one sunny autumn day. I was stranded in the midst of a vast bed of watercress, and just had to stand as the fish swam past me. He turned a little more than a yard below me, midstream, and hung there in some four feet of really strong current with his huge fin up, as well as all the other fins he could muster. Time seemed to stop as we stared at one another through the crystal-clear water, but it could only have been a few seconds before the hook pulled out.

The sexes are less easily distinguished in grayling than in trout but the dorsal fin is often a useful guide. If male and female grayling are examined side by side it will be noticed that the backward projection of the tip of the dorsal fin is greater in males than in females.

Many fishes have a second main dorsal fin behind the first, that is, nearer to the tail. In salmonids, and this is one of the distinguishing marks of the family, this second dorsal fin is greatly reduced in size and often consists only of a short stump of tissue; hence its name of adipose fin (meaning a fin composed of fatty tissue). On the belly side below the adipose fin is a fairly large anal fin, so called because it lies immediately behind the anus. Like the dorsal fin, its rôle is not so much forward propulsion as the maintenance of correct position in the water current. The remaining fins of trout and grayling occur as two pairs, and they are indeed the evolutionary precursors of the paired limbs of other vertebrates – the wings and legs of birds and arms and legs of humans. Both pairs are attached to the sides of the fish and are rather like the twin bilge keels of some racing yachts. The pair nearest the tail lie just ahead of the anus and are termed the pelvic fins (some books simply refer to them as ventral fins, because they lie more or less on the fish's belly). The other pair, positioned one on either side of the body behind the gills, are termed the pectoral fins (pectoral refers to the chest). These pectoral fins are able to perform many different rôles, such as slow forward or backward propulsion, or sideways stabilisation. If your dentist provides such a tranquilliser, have a look at the guppies and goldfish in his aquarium and watch the ways in which they use the pectoral fins. Even fish that are apparently completely stationary are usually moving these fins, often quite vigorously.

Another very obvious external feature of most fish is the body-covering of scales, and salmonids are well endowed with scales. True scales are absent in the non-bony fishes, such as sharks and rays, and very tiny in some species such as eels. Scales overlap one another as do tiles on a roof, indeed the greater part of each scale is covered by the neighbouring scales. A fish's scales perform much the same function as the armour of a fourteenth-century knight, only more efficiently. That is, they provide a tough outer protective layer but permit movement. If a trout or grayling had a continuous layer of outer covering of the same material as scales they would find it impossible to make their graceful streamlined movements through the water. Each scale is a bony outgrowth of the skin and grows as the fish grows – hence their use in determining a fish's age. The slime or mucilage covers the outside of the scales so we can think of a fish as having a covering of thin stiff plates or tiles, all overlapping, with a generous layer of protective goo on the outside. If you have caught a small fish and intend to return it to the water, you should be exceedingly careful not to remove any scales, since patches of fish skin deprived of slime and scales are readily attacked by bacteria and fungi. Fish can regenerate lost or damaged scales but the new ones grow very slowly.

Trout have much smaller scales than grayling. You may even contemplate eating a well-browned trout skin, but no one in his gastronomic senses will attempt to chew grayling skin. Not twice, anyhow! Even my cat Toby leaves grayling scales alone, but will hungrily eat scraps of cooked trout skin. Grayling and sea trout have bright silver scales on their sides, and you may be interested to know that this silver colour is due to the reflection of light from tiny crystals of guanine which are embedded in the scale. In fact guanine is removed from the scales of some very silvery fish such as bleak for use in the manufacture of artificial pearls. The red, yellow and black colours in the trout scales are actual pigments contained in pigment cells called chromatophores. By contracting or expanding the distribution of the pigment the fish is able to alter the intensity and distribution of its colours. That the fish colour is largely determined by what it sees can be proved by covering a fish's eyes and noting its skin colour. Within a few hours, artificially-blinded trout in an aquarium become light and golden – that is, they fail to darken their skins even if living in a dark background. In the wild, as we have all noticed, brightly-coloured fish tend to come from sandy bottoms, dark fish from rocky or weedy bottoms. The silver colours of grayling and sea trout, and also of the Loch Leven strain of the land-locked brown trout, are not the result of pigment but of light refraction by the guanine crystals in the scales. So too are most of rainbow hues of the rainbow trout.

Many fish acquire special colours for the breeding season, and this is especially evident in the trout. The fish tend to darken and become slightly reddish in the late autumn. Grayling, too, take on a darker hue in February before spawning. Some stillwater fisheries continue to use the 'steelhead' rainbow as a stock fish. This rainbow is a spring spawner and when fishing these waters early in the season it is not uncommon to catch very blackish and poorly-conditioned fish. These are most frequently newly spawned cock 'steelhead' rainbows still in breeding colours.

While we are on the subject of scales, we can take a few minutes to consider the ways in which these little pieces of armour-plating can be used both to identify and to age the fish which we have caught. First the identification. As shown in

Fig. 2.2, we should count the number of scales lying between the adipose fin and the lateral line, providing we count in a slightly backward direction from the tail-side of the adipose fin down to the lateral line scale (of the lateral line, more anon). The actual number of scales is of great value in distinguishing between large sea trout and smallish salmon. Whereas *Salmo*

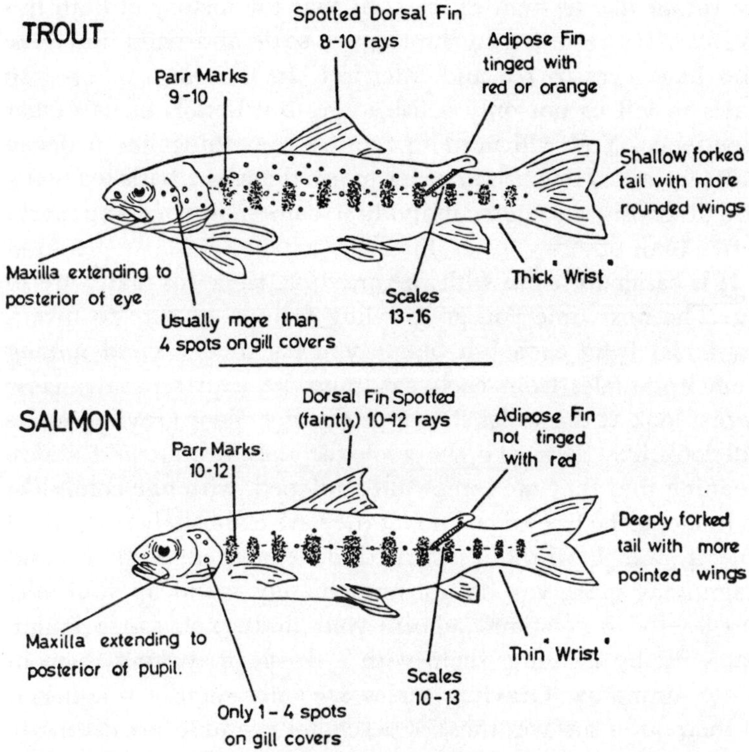

Fig. 2.2 Comparison of trout and salmon parr. The characteristics which are useful in distinguishing the adult *Salmo trutta* and *Salmo salar* include the scale count (position of line of scales from lateral line to adipose fin used in the count is indicated), the thickness of the 'wrist' at the tail insertion, and the degree of forking of the tail.

salar, the salmon, may have anything from 11–15 scales in this row, the sea trout will have a count of 14–19. There is, of course, an unfortunate overlap in the 14–15 scale range but salmon with more than 14 and trout with less than 15 are very unusual, so in general the scale-count proves a reliable guide. It can even be used to distinguish salmon parr and young trout, but here the count is a little more difficult since the scales are much smaller.

Now let us discuss the use of scales for the ageing of fish. Scales are rather like sections of trees, in that the history of both fish and tree are recorded in the rings of scale and trunk for those who have eyes to see and interpret. In fact we can use fish scales to tell us not only a fish's age, but details of its earlier experience. You will need to remove something like a dozen scales from any one fish in order to use them as a basis for really firm diagnosis, since some individual scales show rings and marks better than others.

It is easier to begin with the grayling, since his scales are so big. The next time you go grayling fishing, be sure to take a few scales from each fish before you fry them. Avoid mixing them up; scales from each fish must be kept separate. Now have a look at the scales shown in *Fig. 2.3*. Your grayling scales will look like these. To the zoologist they are ctenoid scales, meaning that they are somewhat scalloped, with fine comb-like teeth along the free edge. In fact they are exquisitely sculptured objects and I will be surprised if, equipped with a hand magnifying glass, you do not immediately round up your wife and family to view and admire your finds. You can brighten scales up by cleaning them with a brush or soaking them in dilute ammonia. Grayling scales are only slightly roughened on their outer surface; those of perch, for example, are distinctly spiny and render these fish very rough to the touch. When using a hand lens to view the scales I find it best to hold each scale up to the light with a pair of forceps – your wife will have a pair for plucking eyebrows in that manicure set you gave her, but if you are one of the lucky ones you will remember having given your son a small microscope for Christmas some years

Fig. 2.3 Photograph of a highly magnified grayling scale, showing the growth rings and probable spawning mark.

ago. Dig it out of the attic and place your scales under it on a glass support slide. Now you are really in business. You will be able to make out the individual chromatophores (pigment cells) in the exposed part of the scales, each one carrying pigment of a particular hue, some contracted into tiny dots, others expanded in spider-like form to maximally display the pigment. Notice, too, the complete absence of chromatophores from the covered area of the scale.

You will see that the scale surface is composed of roughly concentric rings or ridges, but do not leap to the conclusion that each ring represents a year's growth – that would make your grayling about seventy-five years old! Many rings are laid down in one year, but in winter, when the fish tends to grow more slowly, the rings are tightly packed, whereas in summer the rings are widely spaced, indicating fast growth. So you must sort out the concentric rings into year groupings, each year consisting of a summer plus a winter – growth normally begins in early spring. You can even tell good summers from bad by the extent of the fish's growth in that year, and in fish which do not spawn every year, spawning years can be distinguished from non-spawning years. Look at a few scales from the same fish before you make up your mind about age; sometimes you have to take an average, since some scales seem to have an unrepresentative pattern. Make sure you count to the edge of the scale. In old fish, a whole year's growth may be hidden at the outer edge of the scale.

Let us now turn our attention to the scales of the trout. Unfortunately, at least for purposes of our detective work, they are much smaller – about a tenth of the size of the grayling scales (*Fig. 2.4*). They are also much less pretty, being unscalloped and more or less oval in shape. Even the chromatophores are less easily seen. It is best to select scales from a silvery part of the fish where the pigment will not obscure the rings to any extent. These trout scales are not at all hairy and are termed cycloid scales. But the growth rings are still there for the discerning eye of the intelligent angler, and since trout have a more varied life than grayling we can read more

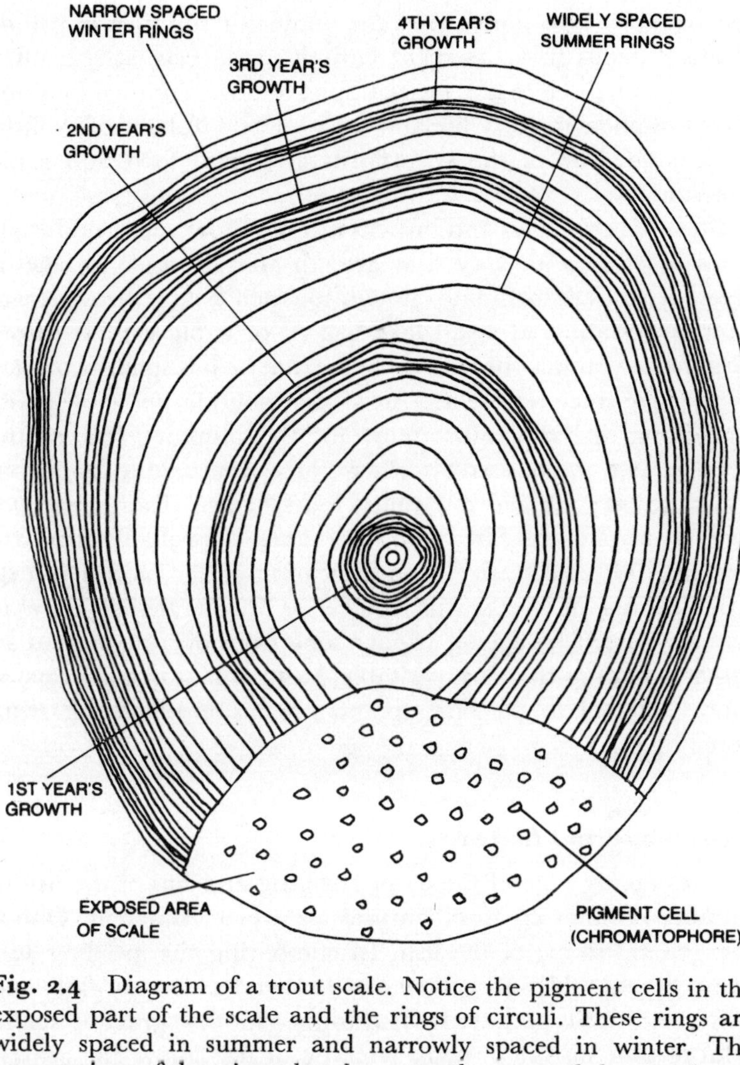

Fig. 2.4 Diagram of a trout scale. Notice the pigment cells in the exposed part of the scale and the rings of circuli. These rings are widely spaced in summer and narrowly spaced in winter. The narrow rings of the winter band are together termed the annulus or annual growth mark.

fascinating detail into our scale-ring analysis. If the fish is a sea trout we will notice that the winter or summer transition is less obvious in years spent entirely or largely at sea, often year two or three of life, for example, and the contrast between river summers in early life and sea summers in later life will be noticeable. Life in the sea affords abundant food and rapid growth.

Stew-fed rainbows and browns usually show very rapid early growth, often with very slow growth after transfer to lake or river. If you are fortunate enough to catch a large brown trout from an established small lake fishery or a big rainbow from Grafham, you may be pleased to see that he has spent two years in the lake since release as a stew-bred pounder, now weighing something like 3 or 4lbs; more for the rainbow, less for the brown. As I emphasised elsewhere, browns are quite long-lived fish and may survive to twenty years of age. Rainbows over five years old are rare, and the same is probably true for grayling. Of course, size is no indication of age, and if you go trout fishing in the Scottish burns or Devon becks you may amuse yourself by ageing 10-inch long trout of little more than ½lb and finding they are veritable Methuselahs of ten years or more! Life is hard in these upland streams and food is hard to come by.

Other external features

Besides taking note of the outer covering and fins of the fish, a number of other external features are worth comment. One is the general shape of the fish. In comparing the grayling and trout, we should notice how the former has a very flattened belly, and this is perhaps related to the fact that grayling spend a lot of time on the bottom, lying on or just above the gravel. By contrast the trout, which is much rounder in section and more torpedo-shaped, is a midwater animal and nearly always on the fin.

Then the general dimensions of head and body can tell us quite a lot about the fish, especially with trout. You may be interested to look at the average length of brown trout at the end of their third year of life in British waters (*Fig. 2.5*). If you are mathematically minded, you may also induce rest on a sleepless night by pondering on the average weight to length ratio of a trout. If expressed in grams, the weight equals 0.01 over the length in centimetres, cubed. I have graphed this on *Fig. 2.6.* From this graph it can be seen that on average a fish of ½lb will be about 10 inches long, a 1-pounder almost 14 inches, a 2-pounder 17 inches and a 3-pounder about 20 inches. Very well-conditioned fish will be shorter than average for their weight; old or hungry trout will be too long.

Then again the time of year will influence a fish's condition very considerably. As is discussed in Chapter 3, both trout and grayling will be somewhat lean in the spring after spawning, coming to peak of condition in June or July, and then heavily swollen with milt or eggs from September onwards. The general dimensions of a fish may also be affected by its sex, especially the comparative proportions of the head. Grayling have small heads, as do many female brown trout, especially top condition female sea trout or 'Loch Leven' browns. By comparison, rainbows have fairly substantial heads, and cock fish (males) almost always have more massive heads than hens (females). The large head of an old male trout is accentuated at or near the breeding season by the upturning of the lower jaw to form a neb. Such an appendage is, of course, even more conspicuous in breeding cock salmon.

Not only is the head of the grayling smaller than that of an equivalent sized trout, but the jaws of the trout meet almost exactly, whereas the upper jaw of the grayling forms a pointed extension over the smaller lower jaw. I have never been able to understand that oft-repeated assertion that grayling have 'soft' mouths. The lips of a grayling are every bit as firm and gristly as those of a trout, and I imagine they are often lost because fishermen are afraid to strike sufficiently firmly to bury the hook over the barb.

Apart from the sense organs which we will discuss in a moment, the only other obvious external feature which we

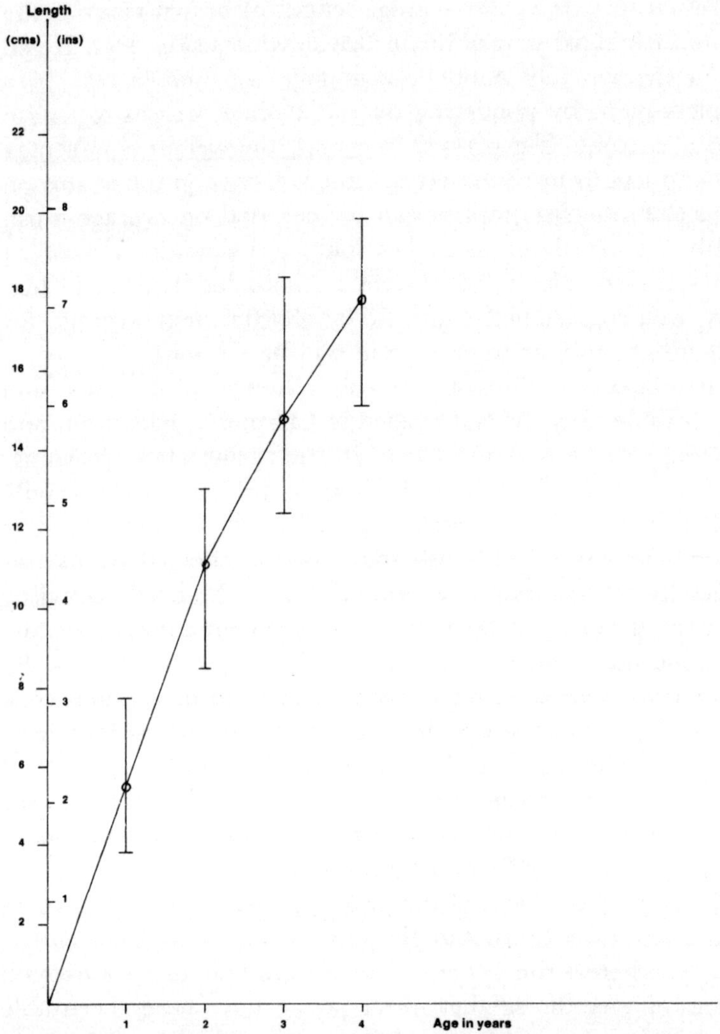

Fig. 2.5 Wild brown trout in lakes and streams. Average length of brown trout of different ages. Range of size is indicated by vertical lines. The rate of growth would normally tend to flatten off after 4 years. It should be noted that in extreme conditions trout may grow much more slowly than these deviations indicate, while fish in chalk streams or stew ponds may grow at up to four times this rate.

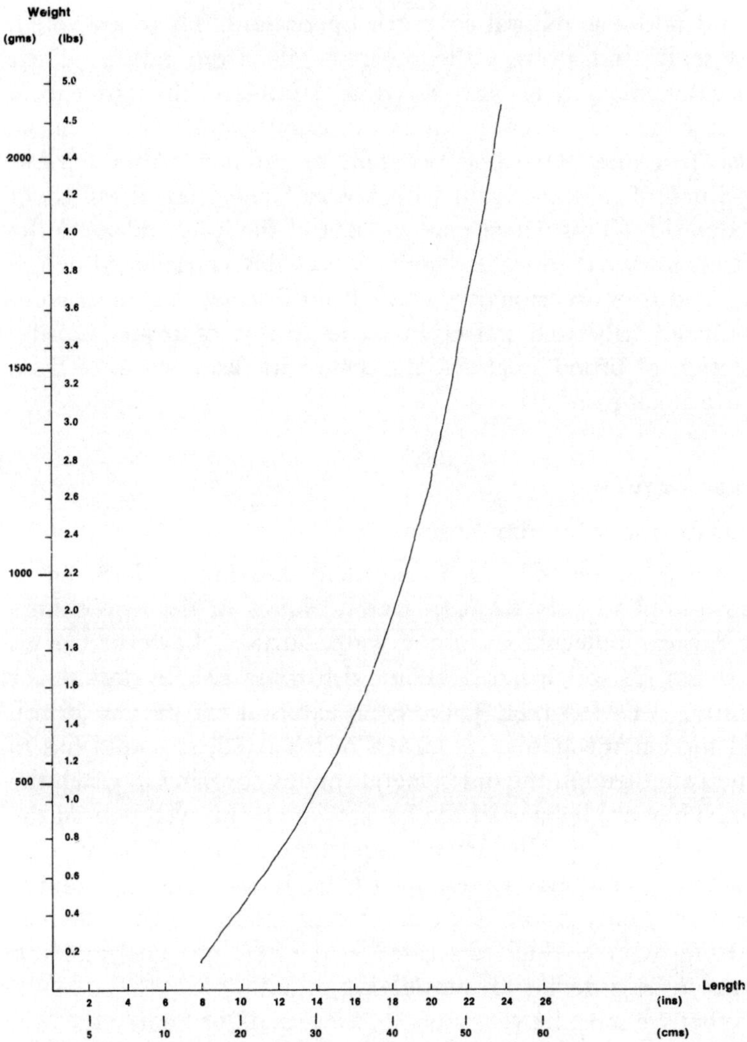

Fig. 2.6 Average relationship between size and weight for healthy trout.

should notice is the gill cover, or operculum. These are tough and scaly and protect the delicate gills from injury. Their muscular movement also helps to stimulate the current of water which continually enters the mouth and flows over the gills. You may have had occasion to catch a rather curious specimen of rainbow trout with a very foreshortened gill cover on one side. This defect exposes part of the gills and gives the fish a somewhat unsightly appearance. But actually, although the condition occasionally results from disease, it is most commonly an inherited defect in some strains of trout. Careful selection of brood stock should ensure its disappearance from future stock fish.

Sense organs

Hearing and vibration sensing

Most freshwater fish have excellent hearing and sound is transmitted rapidly through water. Noises in the atmosphere are largely reflected from the water surface, however, so we need not be too worried about disturbing fish by talking or winding a fishing reel. There is no external ear present in fish and the ear mechanism is buried in the head, so sound has to penetrate through the outer membranous covering to reach the ears. They are located at the back of the head, well behind the eyes, where they also act as important organs of balance in much the same way as our own ears. In some fishes, notably the carp family, there is an inner connection between the ear and the swim bladder (discussed in the next chapter) and this seems to be a device for amplifying sound.

What we must be very alert to, as we stalk or quarry the fish, is his acute ability to detect vibration. This is accomplished partly by the ear, but chiefly by a series of sensory pits and canals beneath the skin. These organs are abundant in the head and also make up the conspicuous lateral line organ, visible in both trout and grayling as a row of modified scales running about the mid-line from head to tail. You may think it resembles a 'Plimsoll line', but its purpose is not to indicate the water line but to alert the fish to your presence as you stomp around the bank or shallows in your waders. Both trout and grayling are very skilled at detecting vibration so a stealthy approach is vital whether we are in or out of the water. This is also the mechanism by which fish detect disturbance in the water, which explains the frequency with which trout can detect flies behind them in still water. Assuming the flies land with something less than the delicacy of thistledown, trout may turn and take such flies – or of course they may alternatively take off for the depths in fright! – so beware the fish's sensitivity to vibration; it is rather better than your own.

It seems probable that fish excite one another by their movement in the water, so that a fish being played after hooking is likely to dissuade other fish from feeding, while a fish actively feeding or rising to feed may encourage such behaviour in other fish. Certainly I have often seen shoals of rainbows indulge in a sudden feeding or hunting frenzy if one of their number finds food, though to what extent such behaviour is truly wild is open to speculation.

Smell and taste

Fish have a well developed sense of smell and taste, centred on the nostrils which are fairly obvious small pits lying ahead of the eyes. Water passes into the nostrils and is monitored by a so-called olfactory pit buried in the head.

In trout fishing, even when worming, the sense of smell is probably not very important, but it is likely to be operative, at least to some degree, when bait fishing for grayling in slow water. Is it just my imagination that recently-impaled maggots catch more fish than maggots which have been thoroughly washed by prolonged use? It seems just conceivable that taste is involved in this type of fishing and that moderately frequent changes of bait are to be recommended.

Sight

There can be no doubt that vision is far and away the most important sense in providing a fish with awareness of its environment and especially so in its feeding behaviour. This is of course not true of eels and some other fish which predominantly hunt by smell, but all the salmonids have very well-developed eyes and hunt very largely by sight. So it will pay us to spend a little time and energy trying to understand how and what our quarry can and does see.

Firstly let us discuss colour vision. It can be stated fairly dogmatically that most fish, including salmonids, have colour vision in good light. The fighting behaviour of the Siamese fighting fish and the male stickleback can be elicited by fish-shaped models with red breasts, but not with such models painted in other colours. Similarly, fish in an aquarium or pond can be trained to show feeding preference for food of a particular colour when offered the same food in a variety of hues. So there need be no question about the ability of trout and grayling to detect the varied colours of flies and lures offered to them. Of course, the problem of detecting the colour of flies sitting on the surface film, or of white or green floating lines, is more complicated and more difficult to resolve. But sunken flies, baits and lures will be seen by trout and grayling in colour, provided the water is reasonably clear. There are some other constraints on colour vision in water. In deep water, colour vision will be distorted both by the general lack of light and by some alteration imposed by the absorption of red light by the water. Although some fish, including trout, may feed actively in darkness (though probably not in complete darkness), it is highly unlikely that colour preference plays any great rôle in choice of prey or fly in partial darkness.

So much for colour vision. Now what about sunlight? Does bright sunlight improve or impair the vision of a fish? I think that there can be little doubt that bright sunlight does not make precise visual definition easy for the fish, especially when we remember that fish have no eyelids with which to shield their eyes from the sun. There is too much glare and glitter both from irregularities of the surface film and by objects in the surface. Some years ago I belonged to a subaqua club and often used to swim down into a rocky sea hole and look back up through the swinging tassels of seaweed to the other world of the water surface, the land and the sky. On a dull day the water surface looked flat and leaden. Objects in the air were visible as vague distorted images only, but objects in the surface film could be discerned with great clarity. If the day afforded bright sunlight, however, the underwater world was lit by a brilliant trembling light while the surface was a dazzling pattern of sun sparkle. Some objects on or in the film were sharply defined by a halo of brilliant reflected light; others were all but invisible because of the broken images of diffracted light. Objects in the air were visible only in sudden flashes, the images for the most part lost in the blinding shaft of reflected light.

When we are concerned with trout or grayling in fast-flowing streams or even rippled stillwater, I would suggest that the fish has rather poor vision in bright sunlight. Other observations confirm this view. I personally find, and others have remarked on similar experiences, that both trout and grayling are most easily frightened or put off the feed when cast over in grey dull light rather than bright sunlight. For my money, you are more likely to be seen clearly by your prey on a dull overcast afternoon than on a bright sunny one or, of course, in the dusk. What goes for you, goes for your fly. You can probably expect the discriminatory powers of the fish to be best on dull afternoons and that is when most changes of fly may be logically required.

Now we must ask what a fish can see in terms of the position of the object. Let us for the moment forget about the water surface and just think of the efficiency of vision for different locations around the fish. The eyes are set on either side of the head, of course, but face slightly forwards. Because of the structure of the retina, the sharpest eyesight of the fish is to the front, and especially in the angular area covered by both eyes. On the other hand, their poorest vision is to the back. Sideways vision is good, and is particularly acute for the detection of movement. If a salmonid wants to scrutinise an immobile object it will examine it head-on (unlike a bird, which will look

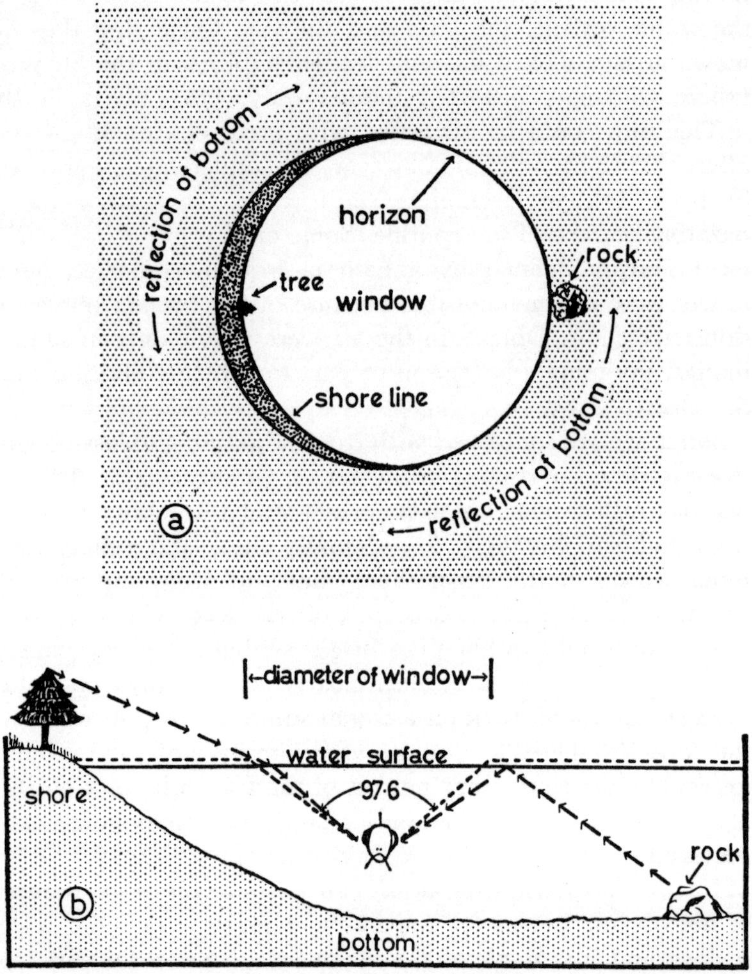

Fig. 2.7 Diagrams to illustrate fish vision above the surface: (a) a diagrammatic representation of what is seen in the aerial window of the fish poised in diagram (b). Outside the angle of 97.6° as indicated, the fish sees a black surround or, in well lit water, a reflection of the bottom.

sideways with one eye when examining an object closely), but objects at the side or behind are detected critically if they move. That is worth a thought as we move up on a feeding fish in midstream.

The next problem to which we must address ourselves is that of the fish's window, as it has come to be called; the area of perception determined partly by bending of light rays as they pass the air water interface, and partly by the effect of reflection on the under side of the surface mirror. As a fish looks upward it sees a round skylight in the surface film, and outside the skylight or window the surface simply reflects back a mirror image of the bottom (*Fig. 2.7*). In order to determine what the fish sees in the window, we must take account of his angle of vision and the bending of the light rays by the surface interface. We find that the combined angle of vision is about 98°. The actual size of the window will vary with the depth at which the fish is swimming. In general, grayling will have a larger window than trout since they tend to cling to the bottom, but presumably the trouts' visual field is clearer since there will be less water disturbance. In practice, what all this boils down to for us, the fishermen, is that we should approach fish from behind whenever possible, keep as low a profile as possible, and not attempt to approach a fish which may be lying in two feet of water within less than five yards. The clarity of a fish's image becomes very poor for objects low on its horizon, so if you can keep down, kneeling if possible, and have some screeen of trees or vegetation behind you, you will have the best chance of not being detected.

3
Some Basic Biology – Internal

Like many another youngster, when I was small I had the general impression about animals that, while they were fairly neat and tidy on the outside, inside they were a mess. My attempts to impale earthworms on hooks, or to gut fish, did little to contradict this view of life. Now I am not going to suggest that any of you, my adult and enlightened readers, would for a moment share in that childish concept of animal biology, but it is just conceivable that somewhere, in the recesses of your mind, some similar thoughts linger on. So let me state at the outset that animals are very deceptive in that what appears when squashed to be just a nasty mess is, in fact, extremely highly organised and structured. Indeed, the very cells of which all living tissues are composed are themselves highly structured, being divided up into many distinct compartments. After all, each cell carries in some of its compartments molecules which, if they leaked to other parts of the cell, would destroy it within seconds. Similarly, the various tissues and fluids of our body must be meticulously separated to ensure our survival. Let us then take a look at the inside of a fish and see what we find.

Muscle

We can do worse than begin with the neat and tidy bits. The largest part of a fish's body is made up of muscle and, of course, that is the edible portion. As we will all have observed, it varies somewhat in colour. Most of the muscle of a trout or grayling is commonly white, and that is actually what it is called by the anatomist – white muscle. There is also a little dark-coloured muscle which becomes brown after cooking. This is distributed immediately beneath the skin in trout and grayling, and is just as edible as the white muscle. It is termed red muscle, being pigmented by a colourful substance called myoglobin, and is present, for example, in the flight muscle of the pigeon, making pigeon breast a delightful delicacy.

The so-called white muscle may itself be pigmented, at least in the trout, often being distinctly pink in colour. This pink flesh is particularly a feature of sea trout, many rainbow trout, and some loch and lake strains of brown trout. The development of this pink colour is often ascribed to a diet of crustaceans, shrimps or prawns and this may well be true, since the carotene pigment which colours the muscle pink is abundant in crustaceans. It is not by any means certain that this colour also indicates a specially pleasant flavour, and maybe that is another of those food prejudices such as the favoured brown egg of the domestic hen. Perhaps we should all do culinary experiments by being fed blindfold with pink- and white-fleshed trout in order to test our ability to discriminate on grounds of flavour. If this book ever runs to a second edition, I shall perhaps be able to report back on such a survey! Of course, there is no doubt that salmon and sea trout are both strongly pink-fleshed and highly flavoured, but that scarcely proves the correlation.

When we come to eat our fish, we cannot help but notice that the muscle occurs in separate blocks. These are termed myotomes and it is the rhythmic contraction of successive blocks of muscle which provides the sinuous body movement of the fish. Notice also the small blocks of muscle that are associated with the bases of the dorsal and ventral fins; this musculature is feeble compared with that provided to operate the caudal fin. You may be interested to know that when, in the evolution of vertebrates, a movement to the land occurred, this rigid subdivision into myotomes proved to be inefficient and was lost. But curiously it still perissts in the embryos of most vertebrates. An early chicken embryo or a larval frog exhibits clear myotomes of muscle in the early body and tail region alongside the developing backbone.

Bones and skull

The salmonids are one of many families of bony fishes, the so-called Teleosts. These fish are quite distinct from the more primitive cartilaginous fishes; the sharks, skates and rays. But compared with such fishes as pike and carp, trout and grayling have relatively few bones and are therefore more desirable for the table. Indeed, unlike ourselves, there are no true bones associated with the internal attachment of the limbs, so the bony parts of a fish are essentially the skull and the bones attached to the backbone. By judicious dissection after cooking, it is comparatively easy to separate flesh from bones, finally lifting out the backbone and with it the entire skeleton of our fish. One of the agonising tribulations of the successful fisherman is to serve up his tasty catch to a guest who proceeds, with the aid of knife and fork, to reduce the whole fish to a mixed stew of flesh and bones which is then scarcely edible. No wonder folk think that the insides of animals are a mess! *Fig. 3.1* illustrates the bony skeleton of a trout; that of the grayling is not dissimilar.

The skull itself deserves some discussion, partly because it is bony and partly because it includes other bony appendages such as teeth. We are particularly concerned with the skull of the trout and grayling when we come to kill our fish. Both of these fish species are easily despatched by a smart blow to the top of the skull just behind the eyes. All fishermen should carry with them a priest or some other suitable instrument for killing the fish when caught. I find a 10-inch length of stiff rubber, about 1-inch square in section, is light to carry and effective in use.

Now a word about teeth. The trout is immediately recognised as a carnivorous animal by its complement of teeth (see *Fig. 3.2*). Rows of teeth adorn both the outer jawbones, the edge of the palate, and a central ploughshare bone on the roof of the trout's mouth is a veritable arsenal of teeth, sufficient to run a small shark a close second. Even the rather rigid tongue of the trout bears small teeth on its upper surface. By contrast the

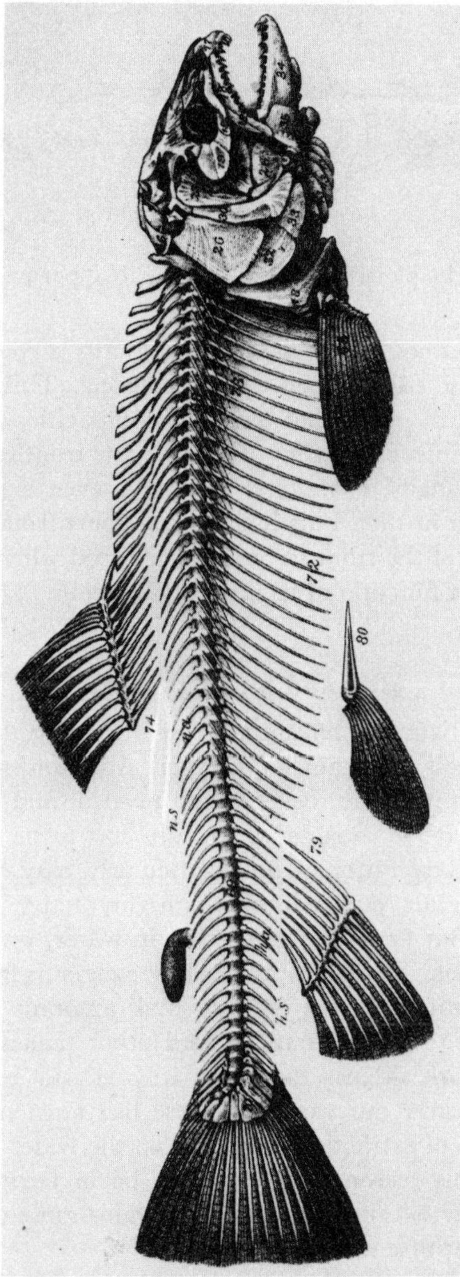

Fig. 3.1 Bony skeleton of a female Loch Leven trout.

Fig. 3.2 The ploughshare bone from the upper palate of a trout.

grayling is almost toothless, possessing only a row of tiny teeth on the outer edge of the upper jawbone. This difference in dentition must imply that trout have capacities to eat types of food impossible for grayling. Probably the trout's ability to deal with large snails, occasional fish, and even small birds and mammals in its diet, puts it in a class apart from the grayling. The ability of the trout to hang on to weed when hooked is no doubt also a function of its armoury of teeth.

Respiration – gills and blood system

Respiration is much more than just breathing. It includes the whole process of acquiring oxygen from outside the body, transporting it to the tissues which need it, and carrying back the waste carbon dioxide which also has to be expelled from the body. Respiration is not particularly easy for an animal living in the air, especially if it is highly active and uses a lot of energy. But for an animal living in water, respiration poses real problems. This is simply because oxygen is freely available in the air but is present only in small amounts as a dissolved gas in water. Yet the muscles and other tissues of trout and grayling work in just the same way as our own and need oxygen to carry out work. So these fish must make a highly efficient job of extracting oxygen from the water in which they live. For this reason they prefer to be in fairly fast-running water, partly because such water contains more oxygen and so makes its capture easier.

Let us begin by considering the gills. They are hidden under the gill covers, no doubt to improve streamlining; only very slow-moving aquatic animals have external gills. Water is taken in at the fish's mouth and passed over the gills as it is forced out from under the gill covers. But both trout and grayling do much more than face upstream with their mouths open, letting water pass over the gills! They actively pump water over the gills, each pumping stroke involving closure of the mouth. The gills themselves comprise rows of tiny filaments over which the water must flow. Within each filament is a tiny blood vessel, through which blood cells are passing in a constant stream. As the water moves over the filament, oxygen passes through the filament membrane from the water and into the red blood cells on the other side. One can think of the red blood cells in somewhat crude terms as exerting an attractive force on the oxygen. You may impress your friends by telling them that a rainbow trout can remove about four-fifths of the dissolved oxygen in the water which passes over its gills. In order to accomplish this the 'gill pump' operates on average some ninety times per minute. If the fish needs even more oxygen this rate is not increased; the fish simply enlarges its mouth cavity and so pumps more water over the gill at each stroke.

Now let us discuss the effect of the aquatic environment on the respiration of our fish. Firstly, the state of flow of the water. Of the two, grayling seem to have a greater desire than trout to live in highly oxygenated water. They like to live in fairly fast streamy stretches of rivers, and although they can and do live in lakes, they are much less of a regular lake dweller than the trout. Nevertheless, lake dwelling presumably constitutes an occasional hazard for a trout, since lake water is more prone than river water to become poorly oxygenated. The factors determining the state of oxygenation are many and are discussed in Chapter 6.

Fish respiration at the gills has some important aspects for the fisherman. It not only tells him in what sort of water he may expect to find the fish he wants to catch, but how he may best tire his fish when it is hooked, in order to bring it to the net. It is probable that it is easier to tire a fish hooked in a lake than one caught in fast-running water, simply because the level of available oxygen for recouping the fish's energies is likely to be less. You can think of a newly hooked fish as being like an athletic man who is running from danger. He may set off at a very fast pace, but if he does so, he must slow after a hundred yards or so since his muscles have then used up the available oxygen and he comes to depend on freshly breathed oxygen. His heart-beat will be speeded up and his breathing rate and depth greatly increased. If he tries to sprint for a further hundred yards he will be in a state of collapse after completing fifty. So there is something to be said for hustling a very active trout to the net within the first few minutes, if possible. Of course, constant tension on the line must prevent a fish using its mouth effectively as a gill pump, at least if it is hooked in the front of the mouth. I suspect that fish hooked in the scissors of the jaw can continue to pump water over the gills rather more effectively and may therefore tire less easily. Foul hooked fish, especially those hooked in the dorsal fin, can continue to acquire oxygen very efficiently and we all know how long it takes to play out such fish. Indeed, I have heard it said that a large salmon hooked on the dorsal fin is virtually uncatchable!

To return to our athletic man beating a retreat from danger. What if he decides to set off at a jog? He may then acquire his 'second wind' more or less as he goes and so continue for a long time at a steady rate. I think it must be much the same with a hooked fish. If our trout or grayling is in good condition but starts off by playing things coolly, we must settle down for a much longer tussle, always realising that he may still retain the potential for a sudden dramatic burst of speed.

Before concluding the subject of respiration, I must consider briefly how the oxygen gets from the gills to the tissues where it is needed. The red blood cells are responsible for the transport of oxygen, and they do this job by means of the interesting molecule which gives them their colour; the red blood pigment, haemoglobin. This molecule has a great affinity for oxygen and has the capacity to bind it where it is plentiful – that is in the gills – and release it where it is scarce, in tissues such as muscles which have used up their available supplies. Studies on haemoglobin also explain an interesting aspect of fish life, namely their great preference for somewhat cold water. As is discussed in Chapter 6, fish such as trout or grayling die quickly in warm water, that is, water that is much above 20°C, and more particularly warm stillwater. Part of this strong preference for cold water is simply the higher oxygen concentrations likely to be found in it. But the other aspect is that, unlike many other biochemical processes, haemoglobin actually becomes less efficient as an oxygen carrier as the temperature rises above about 20°C. So fish are caught out in two quite separate ways; in warm water there is less oxygen to be had, and the oxygen-capturing mechanisms of the body work less efficiently. This explains why some artificially stocked shallow lakes lost all their trout population in the hot summer of 1976.

The heart of a fish is located on the ventral (belly) side just behind the gills. It is quite small, firm and muscular to the touch, and has only three chambers compared to the four-chambered heart of man and other mammals. The circulatory system is also less efficient in fish than in mammals, since the blood is pumped by the heart to the gills and, following oxygenation, is then distributed throughout the fish's body. In mammals the blood returns from lungs to heart for a further pumping stroke to speed it on its way to the body tissues.

Excretion – the kidney

Solid undigested material such as plant tissue and snail shells passes through a fish's intestine and is discharged into the water through the anus. But elimination of water and dissolved salts takes a more complicated route. The organ which is responsible for regulating the excretion of water and excess salts is the kidney, only one being present in fish. It is a long dark-red organ situated immediately below the backbone but above the swim bladder, running from behind the head to just before the tail. (Many fishermen insist on scraping out the kidney when gutting a fish on the grounds that its presence imparts a bitter taste to the flesh during cooking. I am very doubtful of this notion, but it is probably wise to remove it as a possible source of bacterial multiplication if the fish is left to lie about unfrozen and uncooked for any length of time.)

The mass of tiny coiled tubes which make up much of the kidney converge into two ureters and those in turn carry the urine to a small bladder situated close to the anus. The kidney is richly supplied with blood vessels since it is the function of this organ to remove water, salts and waste matter from the blood and discharge it to the bladder.

It is interesting to remember that migratory fish such as salmon and sea trout have completely opposite excretory problems in fresh and salt water. When in the sea, the salt concentration of the sea water is higher than that of the blood and the water will tend to be lost from a fish's blood to the external environment through the gills. A sea fish's kidneys must therefore conserve water and excrete excess salt. Conversely, a freshwater fish will tend to gain water through the gills and so the kidney in this situation must conserve salt but excrete water.

Digestion – stomach, intestine, liver and swim bladder

Most fishermen are familiar with the digestive system of a fish because this makes up most of the tissue which is removed when the fish is cleaned before cooking (see *Fig. 3.3*). The less knowledgeable no doubt pass on this chore to their wives! Good fishermen should also be very familiar with the stomach of the fish through examining its contents for clues to the fish's diet. Neither trout nor grayling chew the food, but simply swallow it by raising the floor of the mouth. In swallowing, food is forced through the gullet or oesophagus into the V-shaped stomach. The stomach of both fish is large and thick-walled, and its muscular nature permits its enlargement after a big meal and also the breakdown of food by its muscular contraction. The recovery of food material from the stomach for analysis by the angler is fully discussed in Chapter 5, and

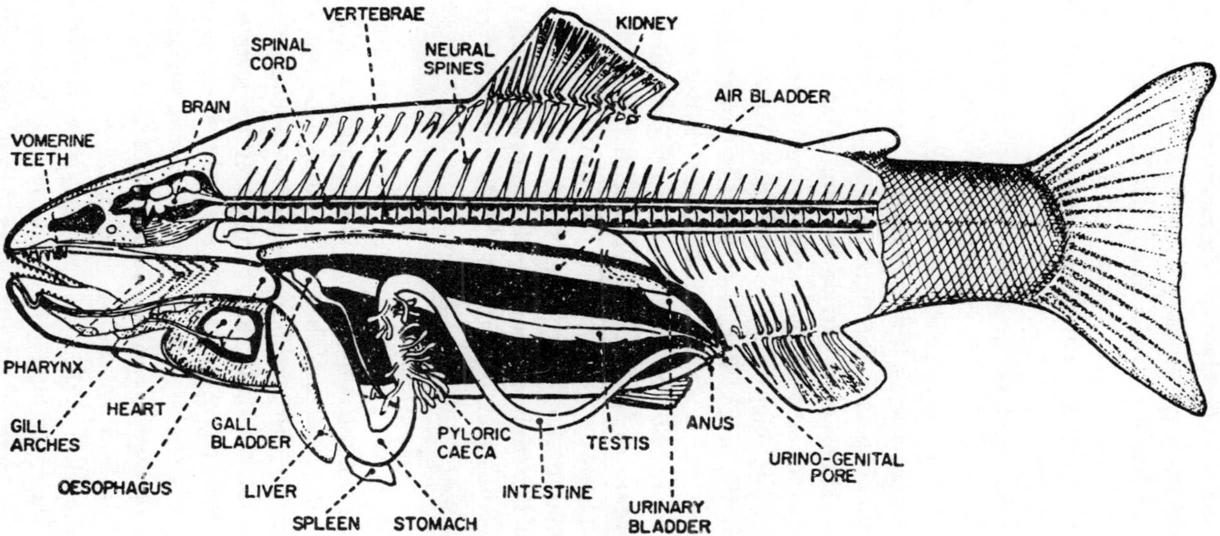

Fig. 3.3 The internal structure of the brown trout, semi-diagrammatic. (Based on Parker and Haswell, 1928)

we need only point out here that digestion proceeds as food passes along the stomach, so only stomach contents from the front portion are likely to yield much useful information for the fisherman. Animals such as worms and daphnia disintegrate rapidly in the stomach and cannot be easily recognised unless recovered very early.

From the stomach, food is passed into the rather short intestine, and here there is no distinct subdivision into small and large intestine as there is in our own alimentary tract. A valve, or sphincter, guards the connection of stomach and intestine and food passes through only when this pyloric sphincter opens. Digestion is carried to completion in the early part of the intestine, assisted by the bile which arrives in the intestine via the bile duct from the small gall bladder – somewhat buried in the liver. The liver itself is brownish-red in colour and lies at the front end of the body cavity beside the stomach. It is normally two-lobed and functions partly as a food storage organ, so its size and appearance provide some indication of the state of health of the fish and the adequacy of its diet. A small organ, brighter in colour than the liver, lies in the crook of the stomach close to the intestine. This is the spleen, the tissue in which old red blood cells are destroyed and some new ones also produced (the liver also functions in this way).

Many fishermen are puzzled by the curious appearance of the outer wall of the intestine, which looks almost as if it were enshrouded by white worms. These long tubules are not worms but so-called caecae, blind tubes attached in a cluster to the front end of the intestine and then lying along its outer wall. I have already remarked on the short length of the fish intestine, and these caecae seem to provide an additional surface area for production of digestive fluids and absorption of already digested materials. Both water and food material are absorbed through the intestinal wall into the bloodstream, although much of this water is later extracted by the kidneys and excreted from the bladder via the urino-genital pore which is located just behind the anus.

This brief discussion of the digestive system will, I hope, suffice to satisfy the moderately curious angler about the fate of the food in trout and grayling and he may also be interested to know that it has been estimated that, at 20°C, midge larvae take some four hours to digest, but snails nine hours. Perhaps that is one reason why fish tend to concentrate on one type of food at a time. To do otherwise may give them indigestion!

There remains for me to mention a really intriguing piece of fish anatomy, the swim bladder. When trout or grayling are being cleaned, the swim bladder is often conspicuous as a transparent air-filled sac, left behind in the body cavity after removal of the gut. It is usually more conspicuous in grayling than in trout. Discussion of the swim bladder under the title of the digestive system is not simply a quirk of the author, for at its front (anterior) end it will be found to be attached to the oesophagus by a short hollow tube, and indeed in embryonic life it commences as an outgrowth from the primitive gut. The amount of gas in the bladder is strictly controlled, so altering the specific gravity of the fish and adapting it precisely to the depth of water at which it wishes to swim. In young trout and perhaps also in grayling, air can be pumped directly into and out of the swim bladder via the oesophageal air duct, and certainly grayling often seem to release bubbles of air when they rise to a fly.

Reproduction – ovary and testes

The breeding behaviour and cycles of trout and grayling are fully discussed in Chapter 4, but here we can usefully mention the location and appearance of the reproductive organs. The ovaries of the female fish and testes of the male are paired, and lie along with the gut in the body cavity. For much of the year both are soft opaque organs, but at all times the ovaries may be distinguished by the presence of small bead-like swellings which represent ripening egg follicles. Since the outer membrane of the ovary eventually ruptures as the mass of ripening eggs increases, hen fish which are close to the breeding season will

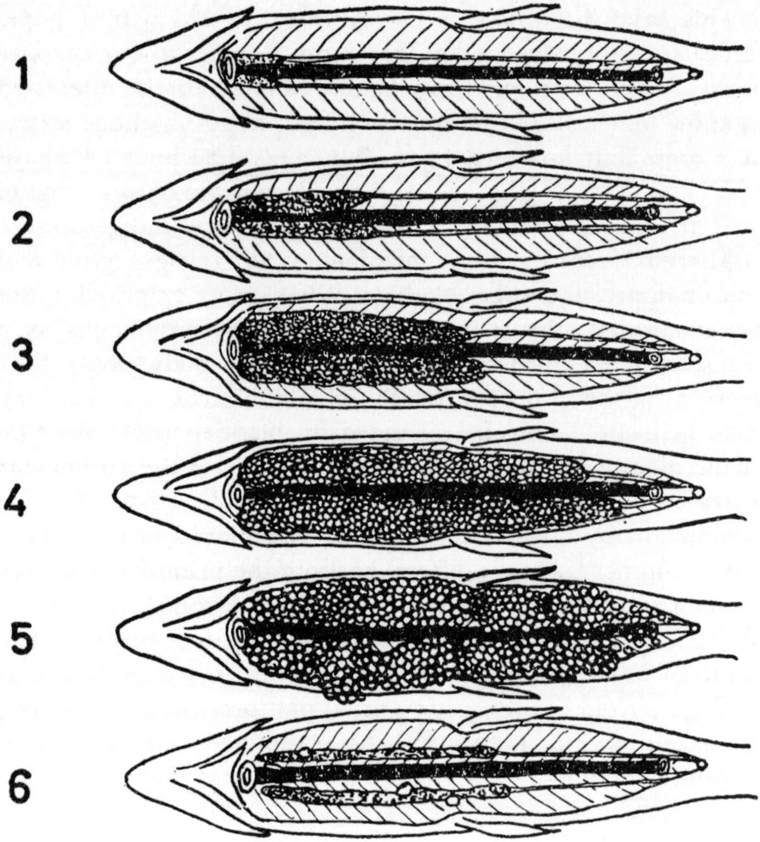

Fig. 3.4 The ovary of a trout in different stages of development.

1 'immature' eggs just visible, has never spawned and will not ripen to spawn at next breeding season;

2–5 'maturing' i.e. ripening to spawn: (2–4 ripening, eggs begin to fill body cavity and grow larger);

5 ripe, eggs ready for shedding, large, free body in cavity. When recovered from spent state a fish is 'mature'. (Diagram from Somme, 1948)

have the body cavity very largely filled with eggs. Following breeding, the ovary of the spent fish looks reddish and pock-marked, the markings representing the old follicles from which eggs have been shed (see *Fig. 3.4*). Ovaries tend to be yellowish or even bright orange in colour.

By contrast, the testes are creamy white (except in spent fish when they tend to be pink) and although large in a ripe cock fish, never fill the body cavity as does the ripe ovary. Both eggs and milt (the fluid extruded by the male, consisting of a suspension of sperm cells) are released from the body through the genital pore, or, more precisely, the urino/genital pore, since the ureters also void the urine through this pore. The pore is located just posterior (nearer the tail) to the anus, and in very ripe fish eggs or milt may be shed from the pore by even, gentle pressure on the sides of the abdomen. Both eggs and sperm are, of course, single cells and both are fascinating to study under a microscope. Sperm and eggs in various stages of development can be found if very small samples of ovary or testes are simply squashed on a slide under a glass cover slip and viewed under the microscope. Staining with a satisfactory biological stain will improve definition but is not essential.

4
Life Histories and Heredity

In this chapter we will discuss the reproduction of trout and grayling, development of the young fish and a few details of the actual mechanism of inheritance.

Breeding behaviour

Both trout and grayling have noticeable but relatively minor differences between the sexes, and since courtship depends primarily on the sexes recognising and attracting one another, this sexual dimorphism is most evident during the breeding season.

Outwardly, the female trout has a smaller and more rounded head than the male, and as the breeding season advances cock fish develop a distinct upturn to the point of the lower jaw, known as a neb or kype. As already mentioned, this feature is most conspicuous in large old trout (it is very well developed in the Atlantic salmon). Distinct breeding coloration also becomes evident as the fish darkens and the pattern of spots becomes more evident. Indeed, even the oft-repeated distinction between brown and rainbow trout – absence of spots from the brown's tail fin – becomes untenable, since spots appear on the tail of the brown trout during the breeding season, especially in male fish I think. Rainbow trout also darken in colour and the magenta splash along the side of the fish becomes more noticeable, contrasting with a splendid iridescent green on the back. Male trout in the breeding season are also more shiny than the female fish.

Compared to trout, the breeding grayling shows few outward changes, apart from the obvious increase in the size of the belly and a somewhat more conspicuous protrusion around the anus and genital pore. The larger and longer dorsal fin of the male grayling has already been mentioned in Chapter 1.

The actual breeding season for brown trout ranges from October to February, and November and December are the commonest spawning months. Variation is apparent between different waters as well as between seasons, and brown trout in the upper Avon (Wiltshire) have the reputation of spawning in February. It is obvious that if a single close season is to apply to all waters, it must extend from early October to late March for brown trout. As has been emphasised in Chapter 1, rainbow of two races are to be found in many places throughout the world. The *shasta* rainbow has a breeding season which tends to overlap with that of the browns, while the *irideus* or steelhead rainbow do not spawn until February or March. Many rainbow fisheries permit fishing throughout October and may also begin the season early, largely on the basis that breeding is not required from the stock fish. But many of the fish caught very late or very early will be found to be in poor condition, being either full of eggs or testis and slightly soft-fleshed, or dark and thin in the spring. There is clearly scope for extending the season in some fisheries, especially stillwater ones, and this could perhaps be most easily achieved by the use of artificially sterilised fish, although I do not know to what extent such fish would still undergo seasonal variation in condition and appearance.

Grayling spawn from March to May, and grayling in excellent condition may be taken between October and February.

The behaviour of the spawning fish is, of course, different from that of the mid-season fish, both in terms of where in the water the fish are to be found and what exactly they are up to. Both trout and grayling spawn in gravel stretches in fairly shallow water – two feet is perhaps an average depth. To find such conditions, trout in lakes or large rivers may ascend even tiny side streams or travel upstream for quite long distances, although trout will spawn in gravelly shallows of lakes if suitable side streams are not available. Since grayling love to live in fast and gravelly stretches of rivers, I imagine that spawning rarely demands a long journey in quest of suitable spawning grounds.

To be honest, I have never actually witnessed grayling in the act of spawning although I have often looked for it. Friends of mine, even river keepers, have been similarly unrewarded. My suspicion is that it is quite rapidly executed and takes place in such fast broken water that observation is difficult. I also suspect that they choose to spawn in slightly deeper water than do trout, and often the spring river water is too coloured to make fish observation easy.

Watching trout spawning is fascinating. Brown trout are sexually highly competitive and aggressive and a number of males may actively compete for one female. The spawning site or 'redd' seems to be selected by the female, and she prepares the site somewhat by moving the pebbles with sideways thrusts of her tail, often turning on to her side for improved efficiency. When actual spawning is about to commence she opens out a trough in the gravel with her tail and then presses her abdomen down into the shallow valley in the gravel, shedding her eggs in amongst the fine stones. Meanwhile one or more males, already in attendance, excrete a cloud of milt from their testes via the genital pore. Milt is simply a mass of motile sperm and fertilisation is completely external, so no actual copulation takes place. The male fish are, however, in close proximity to the female at the moment of shedding the milt, and can often be seen to quiver markedly and sometimes to arch their bodies around that of the female. During the few seconds of spawning both the cock and the hen fish tend to have bellies pressed towards the gravel and mouths widely open. Immediately after one spell of egg shedding, the female makes a few vigorous thrusts with her tail in order to cover the now fertilised eggs with gravel. Such protection is no luxury, for often one can see small trout and other fish gobbling up newly laid trout ova before the female has had a chance to give them a protective covering of gravel.

Artificial fertilisation

Since fertilisation of fish ova is achieved externally, it is comparatively easy to bring about artificial fertilisation by simply mixing eggs and sperm obtained from ripe fish. Gentle but firm pressure along the flanks of ripe fish will lead to expression of eggs or milt. Normally eggs are obtained first and then milt shed over them, followed by addition of clean water. Techniques for the hatching of such eggs and rearing of the young fish are now well established, the chief requirements being a supply of clean pure water, free from silt, at a steady temperature. Water from underground spring sources is ideal, both because its temperature is very stable, and also because it does not carry a suspension of silt, the greatest problem in the maintenance of fish eggs. Grayling eggs have proved more difficult to maintain than those of trout, and in Europe, where grayling culture has been practised for many years, eggs are kept in special glasses (see *Fig. 4.1*) with a steady upward flow

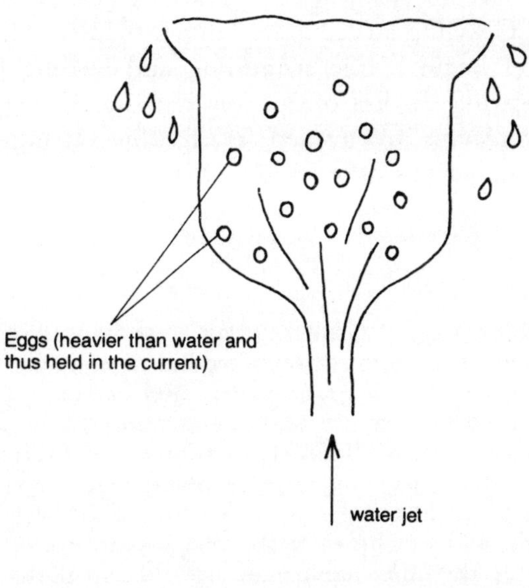

Fig. 4.1 Diagram of a glass used for the culture of grayling eggs.

of water. A few more comments on fish rearing will be found in Chapter 10, but it is a topic on which I am simply an interested observer.

A female trout may lay several thousand eggs depending on its weight; grayling lay many more. In the case of trout the eggs seem to be laid in batches, about 200 or so in each 'nest'. Often one female fish will make successive nests by moving upstream in the same redd after each spawning, the cutting of a new nest helping to send a gravel covering over the freshly laid eggs. Sperm cells will survive in fresh water for only about one minute and each egg is fertilised by only one sperm. Since the eggs are heavier than water and slightly sticky, they readily remain in the gravel, and will hatch in 30 to 100 days depending on the water temperature. It thus follows that a long cold spring may hold up the appearance of new stock by some two months!

The newly hatched fish, termed alevins, possess a large yolk sac, and only when this food store is almost exhausted does true feeding begin. At this stage the mortality of the larval fish is often enormous, since a host of aquatic organisms find them a ready meal. Grayling larvae have a much smaller yolk sac than do trout and begin a free swimming and feeding life much earlier. Following the loss of the yolk sac and the beginning of feeding, the alevins are termed fry, feeding on minute plant and animal material in the water – the microplankton. As fry

Fig. 4.2 (facing page) Growth rates of trout and grayling in different waters. These growth rates are based on actual weights of fish sampled at 1 year, 2 years, or 3 years after hatching. The figures must be accepted as averages, since in extreme conditions growth can be much slower or much faster. Both brown and rainbow trout, but especially the latter, can grow at phenomenal rates in newly formed lakes or artificial stew ponds where food is very abundant and nutritious, and weights of 20 lbs after 3 years are by no means uncommon. On the other hand some streams and burns may have sexually mature fish of 4 years of age weighing only a few ounces.

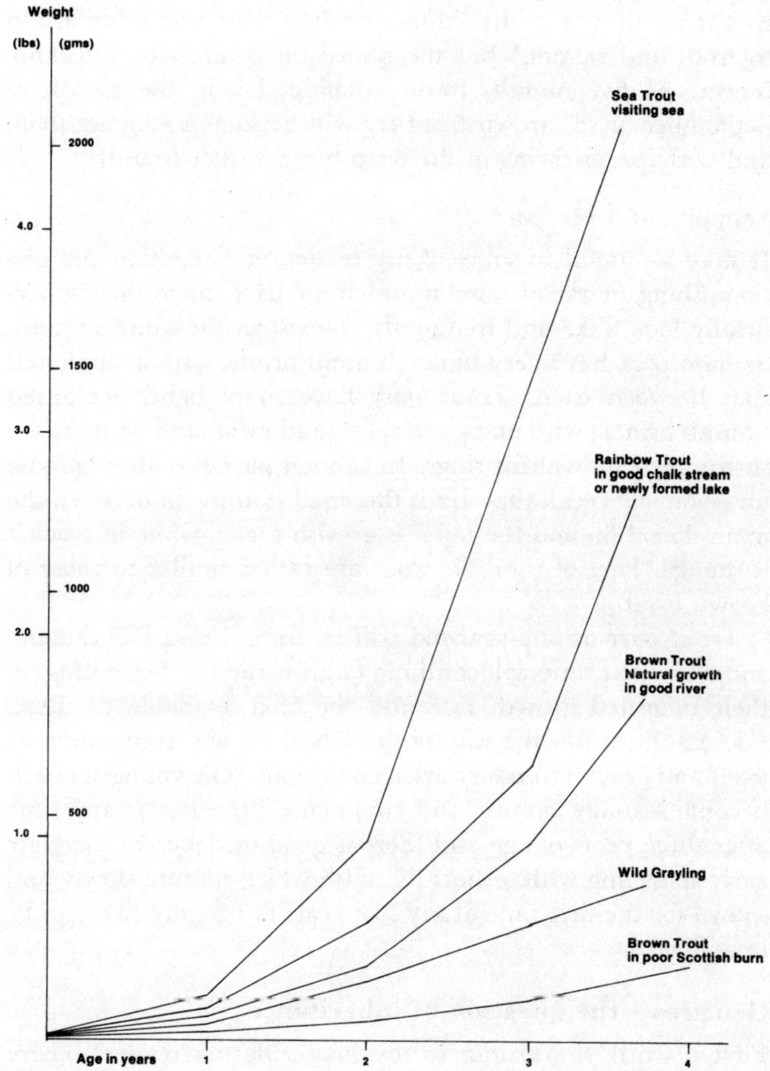

Weight
(lbs)
(gms)
2000
4.0
1500
3.0
1000
2.0
500
1.0
Sea Trout
visiting sea
Rainbow Trout
in good chalk stream
or newly formed lake
Brown Trout
Natural growth
in good river
Wild Grayling
Brown Trout
in poor Scottish burn
Age in years
1
2
3
4

grow they come to resemble the adults somewhat, the trout having the distinct 'thumb prints' along their flanks together with many spots; grayling fry resemble trout fry in possessing spots and 'thumb prints' (thus revealing their true relationship to trout and salmon) but the dorsal fin is already noticeably bigger. At five months from hatching, i.e. in the month of September or so, brown trout fry will be some 2½ inches long, and perhaps deserving of the term 'parr' rather than fry.

Salmon and trout parr

It may be useful to some of my readers if I mention the distinguishing marks of salmon and trout parr, since they superficially look alike and frequently co-exist in the same streams. Salmon parr have very bluish 'thumb prints' with a single red spot between each. Trout parr have more lightly coloured 'thumb prints', with many red spots, and most of these spots are surrounded by whitish rings. In salmon parr the little adipose fin – you will recall that this is the small stumpy fin between the main dorsal fin and the tail – is greyish green, while in trout it is orange. Parr of rainbow trout are rather similar to those of brown trout.

Trout parr at one-year-old will be from 2 to 4 inches long, and from that time will continue to grow rapidly depending on their inherited growth rate and the food available to them. *Fig. 4.2* illustrates the rate of growth of brown trout, rainbow trout and grayling under varied conditions. The youngsters will become sexually mature and commence breeding at any time after three years of age and there is good evidence to correlate early spawning with a short life. Fish which mature slowly and spawn for the first time at say five years of age, are likely to be long lived.

Genetics – the question of inheritance

First a word of warning to my long-suffering reader! There now follows a discussion of inheritance, which many fishermen may find tedious and should skip, although I would like to think that their native curiosity might tempt them to read further. But fish breeders and those interested in fish stocking policies will, I trust, find here something of value. I freely admit that the inclusion of this short section may have something to do with the fact that I am, by profession, a geneticist. But inheritance is such an intriguing subject to all of us who breed fish, dogs, elephants or children that I do not apologise for its inclusion. After all, our children not only resemble human beings rather than elephants, but also resemble their parents more closely than other humans. Moreover, that heritable 'information' was somehow packed into two cells, a single sperm and a single egg. As with us, so with fish. So let us discuss this amazing topic in a little detail.

Nature and Nurture – the eternal riddle

The characteristics of any organism, fly, fish, or fowl, both in terms of anatomy and behaviour, result from an interaction of two influences. These are the influence of genetics (normally termed inheritance) and the influence of the environment in which the animal is reared: these twin factors are often tersely referred to as Nature and Nurture. To illustrate the principle in the case of fish, a group of trout might all be heavily spotted because they are descended from very spotted parents – that is mainly Nature. But fry from the same parents may grow at very different rates in different streams because of variation in food level – that is mainly Nurture. No single character, anatomical structure or aspect of behaviour is entirely determined by inheritance on the one hand or environment on the other. Rather, all are the result of an interaction, but the spotting is *chiefly* Nature and the variation in growth rate *chiefly* Nurture. In many animals it is possible to sort out the separate influences of Nature and Nurture by rearing identical twins of groups of very highly inbred individuals. Any variation between such individuals is then known to be entirely induced by the environment. Identical twins or inbred strains are genetically identical individuals, and this can be experimentally verified by taking a graft of skin from one of the animals and inserting it on the other. Genetically identical individuals accept one another's skin grafts. Unfortunately, because of the external fertilisation which occurs in fish, neither identical twins nor truly inbred strains can be isolated, and, if they could, verification by skin grafting would be very difficult. It is therefore likely that planned fish breeding will remain a slightly chancy business for some time and that selection for particular characters will not be straightforward.

As we now consider how heredity works, let us remember what has been stressed above; namely, that all characters result from an interaction of genetics and environment, and therefore, although we are considering the genetic aspects, most of the characters being considered can be profoundly affected by environmental influences.

How heredity works

Each character which is genetically determined results from the influence of one or more genetic factors called genes. It is now known that a single gene consists of a length of a long string-like molecule called DNA. Some characters are controlled by single genes, others result from an interaction of many genes. A single sperm or egg cell contains one copy of each gene – animals such as fishes and humans probably have between 5000 and 50 000 different genes – and the DNA encoding all these factors is tightly packaged inside these cells. When the sperm and egg cells unite, the fertilised egg now possesses two copies of each gene, one derived from the male and one from the female. In the language of science, sperm and egg cells are haploid, while the fertilised egg and all the cells to which it gives rise (except more eggs and sperms) are diploid. As a result of this union of genes from male and female, there follows a fascinating competition between the two copies of each gene: in the resulting development of the offspring we can witness the outcome of such competition. Sometimes both genes may retain a significant influence and the offspring may demonstrate a compromise between the two influences. At other times the influence of one gene predominates over the other and the resulting character is as if only one type of gene were present.

This phenomenon is called dominance. We are here discussing only the interaction of a pair of genes for one character. The thousands of other genes will also be competing with their opposite numbers, but each independently. So you and I may exhibit in our anatomy the dominance of blue eyes over brown eyes, assuming our mother to be blue-eyed and father brown-eyed, and at the same time the dominance of lobed ears over non-lobed ears, assuming mother to have had non-lobed ears (a problem if she was fond of earrings!) and our father to have had lobed ears.

This brief account of how genes interact has two fascinating implications. The first is that any animal, trout or human, will carry genes which it does not express, for example the gene for brown eyes or lobeless ears mentioned in the imaginary case above. The second implication follows from this, namely that, when the adult animal in turn produces eggs and sperms, only one copy of each gene is donated to each, and so the imaginary individual above will pass on sperms (assuming him to be male!) which carry genes for blue eyes and brown eyes, and lobed ears and lobeless ears. In fact there will be four kinds of sperm in terms of these two characters: blue/lobed; blue/unlobed; brown/lobed; and brown/unlobed.

What, you will now be demanding as you clean out your pipe for the third time, does all this have to do with fish – or even with fish breeding? A moment, my eager reader, and your curiosity will be rewarded. You will, moreover, have joined the small band of those special people who understand something about genetics!

The most important implication of these genetic considerations for those breeding or selecting fish is to realise that their task is not simple. Large fish may not give rise to large fish, nor handsome fish to others of equal splendour. Secondly, interbreeding distinct strains or species of fish may reveal characters in the hybrid stock never expressed in the parents. After all, the tiger trout display a barred zebra-like pattern not revealed by either the brown or brook trout parents. Another important consideration for fish breeding and selection is that the characters which one may be most interested in promoting, such as rapid growth or late sexual maturity, are likely to be affected by many different genes in a genetic interaction, and so we may not expect to see rapid response to any breeding policy based on selection. All the average fish farmer can be advised to do in the short term is to choose well-shaped healthy fish for breeding purposes and to discard fish with malformations. If eggs are bought in, they are best bought from a source whose stock fish are known to be good.

It has recently become fashionable for many farmers to buy in foreign fertile rainbow eggs, imported by air from countries in which breeding commences early. This practise often permits the hatching of the eggs by Christmas or before, so avoiding the long incubation involved in the use of very cold water. At the Houghton Club fishery on the Test, for example, I am told that, using underground water at a steady 11°C., all trout eggs are hatched before Christmas. Such a policy has much to commend it in the short term, but the constant emphasis on fast growth and early maturity may bring with it the penalty of short fish life and a natural death at less than five years of age.

Given that the average breeder can do little more than practise sensible selection, what else could be achieved in the long term? Any of us who are livestock farmers will know that much has been achieved in improving the milk yield or weight gain of cattle by carefully controlled breeding using pedigree stock. Such a programme would be difficult but not absolutely impossible for fish. It would imply the marking of individual fish, both cocks and hens, and isolation of their progeny in separate but comparable ponds or lakes. This requirement harks back to my earlier comments about the interaction of genetics and environment. Unless the rearing conditions are essentially alike, one cannot be certain that differences in the stock are genetically determined. Comparison of progeny over a number of years would lead to the identification of good breeding fish which regularly gave excellent progeny. Such selected fish and some of their progeny would then be isolated and retained as a desirable line of fish with which to breed. In addition, as such lines of breeding fish were developed, crossing between them to give a first generation of hybrids (so-called F1. hybrids) might prove a useful strategy. That, after all, is what happens in farming in the production of the 'half-bred' sheep and the Hereford/Fresian cross beef animal.

Similarly, even if the regular production of such hybrid fish were not to be followed as a regular policy, it is advantageous to occasionally bring some new animals from another line into the breeding stock, since constant selection and inbreeding of one related line of fish is apt to throw up fish with undesirable traits. One common trait often seen in trout is the almost complete absence of one gill cover, a harmless but unsightly development. Excessive inbreeding tends to reveal the expression of recessive genes which would in other circumstances always be repressed.

Some brief reference was made in Chapter 1 to the hormonal treatment of trout as a means of achieving optimal weight gain. From a number of points of view the female trout is a better commercial proposition than the male, since she grows more rapidly, is less aggressive and troublesome to other fish in the same pool, and comes to sexual maturity somewhat later than the male. Feeding of female hormone in the diet will induce feminisation of male trout, but the hormone residues in the tissues of the fish render such fish unsuitable for the table. The laboratory of the Ministry of Agriculture, Fisheries and Food at Lowestoft has recently developed an interesting alternative approach. Female trout are treated with male sex hormone, which induces the progressive development of maleness and even the production of viable sperm. But such sperm will all be female-determining (i.e. only the female X chromosome will be present in such sperm) and so, when it is used for fertilisation of normal eggs, all the progeny will be female. Such fish will be 100 per cent normal females and will have had no contact with hormone fortified diets themselves. They will therefore be ideal fish for use in intensive growth for the table, or for stocking in put-and-take waters.

It may be that the use of artificial sterilisation or hormone therapy to induce weight gain may prove as useful in fish production as they have in livestock farming. Meantime, there is much to be said for the delight of catching a wild ½lb brown trout from a Scottish mountain burn, and things to be said against hauling a 2lb stew-fed monstrosity from some overstocked gravel pit. But perhaps not many of us can afford to be all that choosy about our fishing nowadays!

Chromosomes

Some of you may wonder why I have not mentioned chromosomes of trout and grayling when discussing their species determination and heredity. Chromosomes have often proved useful in distinguishing between similar species or demonstrating relationships between dissimilar species. But the truth is that the chromosomes of salmonid fish are both small and numerous, and afford very little practical help to us in our interest in the breeding and classification of these fish.

5
Pests and Diseases

Pests of fishermen deserve a book on their own for adequate coverage. They include horse flies, midges, bulls, barbed wire, over-zealous keepers, and under-zealous wives. But my knowledge or experience on these topics is, I trust, no greater than that of most of my readers, and no doubt less than some.

This will be a shortish chapter, however, since, fortunately, diseased fish do not bother the game fisherman very frequently. They do trouble trout breeders however, and as fish are reared intensively and heavily stocked on a put-and-take basis, it seems likely that fishermen will encounter diseased fish with increasing frequency in future. But first let me mention in passing, as it were, some diseases, not of fish, but of fishermen.

Diseases of fishermen

Food poisoning

There are two possible sources of food poisoning encountered more by fishermen than by other folk. The chief causative organism is the bacterium *Salmonella* and although an attack is rarely serious it can be inconvenient and uncomfortable. Far and away the commonest source is inadequately cooked fish or flesh. If a fisherman is careless in cleaning his fish and permits the fish gut contents to contaminate the flesh; if the fish is then kept at room temperature for a day or more; and finally, if the fish is inadequately cooked, then, as you can guess, trouble will follow. Trout and grayling are no more likely to cause trouble than any other kind of fish, but beware. Clean the fish properly, keep them cold, and cook them correctly. Indeed, provided the latter is carried out, even negligence on the first two counts will be rectified. But it is best to be safe on all counts.

Another possible source of food poisoning is only likely to affect winter grayling fishermen, for here the maggots are the problem. Since blowfly maggots are flesh eaters, they are very likely to be contaminated with *Salmonella* bacterium, so, to avoid a sore tum, wash your hands before you eat your sandwiches when maggoting!

Botulism

This really nasty disease is caused by a bacterium termed *Clostridium botulinum* or, to be more correct, by a toxic substance released by the bacterium. Although occurring naturally in the gut of many fish, the disease is fortunately very rare. (A recent fatality in the U.K. was attributed to the disease, and traced to a contaminated tin of Canadian salmon.) Precautions are as for *Salmonella*, i.e. careful cleansing, proper freezing and adequate cooking.

Lead poisoning

I insert this possible illness only as an aside. Although I have never heard of a case of a fisherman contracting lead poisoning, it does seem to me a bad idea to close lead shot pellets with one's teeth! Admittedly, lead is very insoluble, but it is also very poisonous and is cumulative. Certainly, if one swallowed a pellet, I would guess that the acid in the stomach would dissolve more than would be thought desirable. So, in my view, use small pliers. But perhaps I am being over-alarmist!

Pests and diseases of grayling

I know of no serious disease affecting stocks of wild grayling. They do harbour many parasites common to trout, but rarely are these present in large numbers to damage the health of the fish. Only one worm has come to my attention at all frequently in grayling, and that is the spiny-headed worm sometimes found attached to the inside wall of the lower intestine. Since it is not in the best interests of a parasite to kill or even to harm its host animal, we should not be surprised to find that fish carrying these worms appear to be perfectly healthy. I may add that these and other worms found in grayling or trout are entirely harmless to man, even if accidentally eaten.

Pests and diseases of trout

Until a decade or two ago, only a very few diseases of trout came to the notice of fishermen, but recently with the advent of heavy stocking and fish farming, trout diseases have assumed a much greater significance. Since this book is not primarily intended for fish farmers, and I am no expert on fish diseases, it will involve only a glance at a batch of diseases that come to the fisherman's notice. A much more detailed account can be found in an excellent book by Dr Ronald Roberts. Dr Roberts, who is a professional fish pathologist at Stirling University, also contributed a series of articles on trout diseases to *Trout & Salmon* magazine during 1978.

Sea louse

This little beastie, although termed a louse, is really a crustacean – a distant relative of crabs and lobsters – and will only be encountered by trout fishermen who are fortunate enough to catch fresh run sea-trout. They are small brown parasites attached to the skin and scales and they cannot survive for more than, at most, 48 hours in fresh water. Their presence is always looked on with delight by fishermen, since they indicate the fish's recent arrival from the sea. In normal events they do little harm to the fish, although the lesions which they make on the skin could be sites for more serious later invasions of *furunculosis* (below) or even UDN (see page 71). But it has been reported that stocks of trout and salmon retained captive in sea tanks build up very large infections of these sea lice, and that they prove a considerable problem to the marine fish farmer.

Gill maggots

These creatures are, like sea lice, crustacean parasites chiefly affecting sea trout and salmon, but whereas sea lice indicate a fish's recent arrival from the sea, the presence of gill maggots can be taken to imply a previous spawning visit to fresh water by the affected fish. This follows from the fact that the parasites can be contracted only by adult fish in fresh water. Resembling small flattened tadpoles in appearance, these parasites do not inflict really drastic damage on the host fish but result in ragged and messy gills, since they are attached to and feed on the outer fringes of gill lamellae. A heavy infestation must certainly reduce the respiratory efficiency of the host fish.

Furunculosis

This disease is well known to even the oldest fishermen, since it has been a serious scourge of salmonid and other fish for centuries. It was first described in detail in the late nineteenth century, and in 1929 a Royal Commission was set up by the House of Lords to investigate the disease as a result of its disastrous effects on fish stocks in rivers such as Tweed and Spey. Basically the disease is caused by a bacterium called *Aeromonas salmonicida*, a name which suggests that only salmon or salmonids are affected by it, which is incorrect; many other fish species may also suffer attacks. Although the bacterium resides for much of the time in the kidney of the fish, its most noticeable effects during an outbreak are the ugly patches or *furuncles* on the skin. In the later stages these lesions exude blood-stained fluid. Diseased fish should be removed from the water as quickly as possible by keepers or fishermen, since their removal before rupture of the furuncles will do much to limit spread of the disease. The disease spreads most rapidly in conditions of high water temperature, and rainbow trout seem to be less prone to attack than brown trout. *Furunculosis*, like UDN, is a notifiable disease.

Eye fluke

Like *furunculosis*, this disease is by no means uncommon and is one of the most serious problems of both trout farmers and fishery managers. Caused by a parasitic fluke, *Diplostomum spathaceum*, the disease affects the trout by the accumulation of larval flukes in the fish eye, especially the lens, and fish carrying a heavy infestation become blind. Most frequently the affected fish caught by fishermen are only partially blind, but obviously the totally blind fish will not survive. Infected fish can sometimes be seen swimming close in to the shore line of a lake, and are normally very dark in colour since visual signals are required to initiate normal colour adaption to the environmental background.

It is obviously arguable whether partially blinded fish are more or less difficult to catch than fully sighted ones. Provided the fish has not lost condition, trout with a few eye flukes are perfectly edible and probably suffer little from the attack.

Like many flukes, this parasite has an interesting if complicated life history, involving not only the fish but also a bird and a snail. As illustrated in *Fig. 5.1*, what happens is that fluke eggs occur in the droppings of infected fish-eating birds. If the excrement falls on water, the eggs hatch, releasing a tiny swimming larva which seeks out a fresh-water snail and burrows into its tissues. Infected snails continue to thrive normally but now release large numbers of stage 2 swimming larvae. These larvae seek out a fish host, burrowing into its tissues and migrating ultimately to the eye. Within the eye lens the larvae flukes persist until death. If the fish is now eaten, either dead or alive, by a bird – herons, fish-eating ducks and sea gulls are the most frequent species involved – the larvae once more become active and develop into mature flukes in the avian intestine. Thus a new source of fluke eggs is established.

No satisfactory treatment for affected fish is known, and fishery managers usually depend on the discouragement or, if necessary, destruction of bird hosts. Notice that many potential bird hosts such as herons, mergansers, goosanders, and ospreys are protected by law however, and may only be discouraged, not destroyed. Gulls seem to be the most frequent intermediate hosts for the flukes since they feed avidly on dead fish which they may find floating on the fringes of lakes or reservoirs. Some fisheries have attempted to eliminate the snail host,

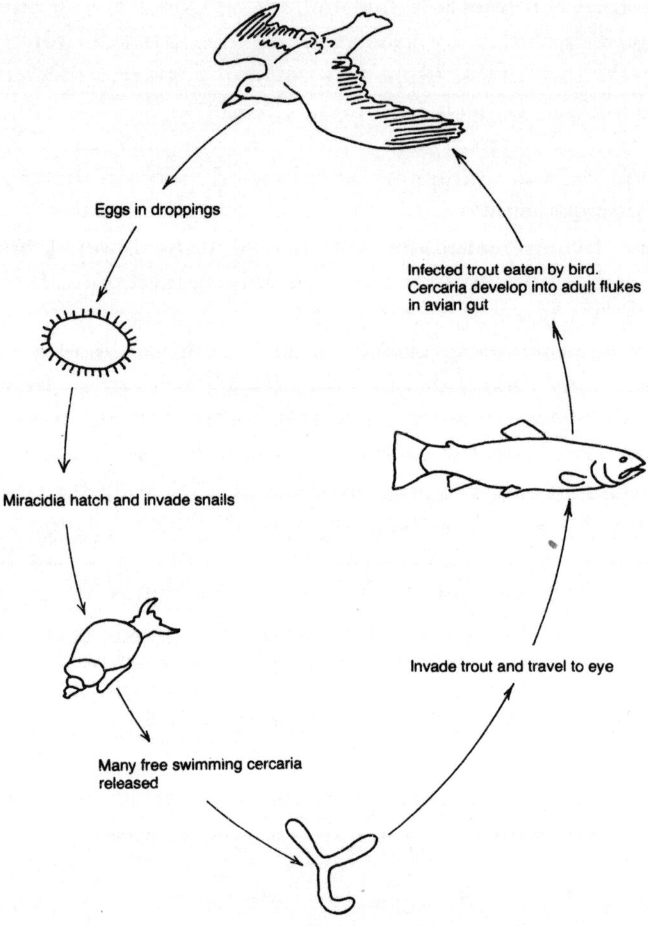

Fig. 5.1 Life history of the trout eye fluke.

but this is often expensive or impossible, and, since snails are themselves a valuable food of trout, inadvisable. Other fisheries, or more precisely, fish farms, with an incoming water supply already contaminated by the cercariae (the stage which leaves the snail and infects the trout), have resorted to an electrode system placed in the intake channel to kill the fluke larvae.

There is some evidence that rainbow trout are more commonly affected than browns and, in affected lakes, some fish seem to harbour very heavy infestations when other fish seem entirely clean. I wonder whether this apparently non-random distribution may depend on the habits of the individual fish, even that fish eating infected snails could be infected by cercariae through the gut wall. It sounds unlikely but just possible, and would imply resistance of the cercariae to the digestive processes. Intestinal parasites do possess such resistance, of course.

A word of advice for fishermen. If you catch a badly infected fish, or find a dead one, never leave it for the gulls to eat. Bury it or hand it to the keeper for disposal. He will greatly appreciate your trouble.

Fin rot

Like eye fluke, fish suffering from the effects of fin rot are most likely to be encountered by those fishing small stillwater fisheries which are frequently and heavily stocked with stew-fed fish. Affected fish at worst can be a sorry sight, since the dorsal, pectoral and tail fins partly disintegrate, leaving exposed spiky fin rays protruding. Such fish are also very poor swimmers and can be hauled to the net like a lump of weed when hooked.

The cause of fin rot is not established beyond doubt, but seems to involve a bacterium termed *Aeromonas*. Infections in trout farms can be treated chemically by the use of suitable anti-bacterial agents such as malachite green. Fishermen may also encounter fish which have incomplete fins without obvious signs of rotting. Such fish have probably been reared in tanks at high density and the affected fin has simply been bitten by another trout!

My impression is that fin rot is very rare in wild trout.

Ich

This is another disease which has become a problem in some trout fisheries simply as a result of fish farming and intensive stocking. It is not confined to salmonids, but is a common disease of coarse fish in the warm waters of southern England and in Europe, and has been known in Continental carp farms for many years. As a disease of trout it is most evident in stocks of rainbow trout in the southern parts of the British Isles. Infected fish are characterised by white spots or pimples on skin and fins, and these spots exude the causative organism of the disease, a single-celled protozoan organism called *Ichthiophthirus multifilis* (from which the disease takes its name). Infected fish seem to be irritated by the presence of the spots and have a habit of rubbing themselves against the bottom and sides of the lake with a characteristic flash of silver belly. Since the parasite persists in the water where infected fish occur, eradication is difficult. Reduction of stocking intensity is almost the only effective control, and spread is most evident in warm summer conditions and low water.

IPN (*Infective Pancreatic Necrosis*)

This serious virus disease of trout was apparently introduced to European waters from the U.S.A. High mortality occurs amongst very young fish at the fry stage, and quoted mortality figures of 85 per cent are common. Unfortunately it is the surviving fish of such epidemics which become symptomless carriers. Such fish seem to be able to shed virus with their eggs and sperm, so infected adults give rise to further batches of infected fry. Although I have referred to surviving infected adults as symptomless that is slightly incorrect, since such fish do seem to be more prone than normal trout to other diseases and the trauma of transportation. Infected fry show viral proliferation and damage in the pancreas and the intestinal wall. A very serious view is currently taken of the threat of IPN disease; it is notifiable, and barriers to movements of live fish are imposed in infected areas.

UDN (*Ulcerative Dermal Necrosis*)

This disease has been much in the news of recent years because of its unfortunate prevalence in the salmon and sea trout stocks of many of our rivers. It seems to be confined to adult fish and to make its first appearance as the fish enter fresh water on their spawning run from the sea. Most evident in the cold winter months, the disease can be first detected as small pale grey patches on the sides of gill covers and snout. These pale patches then spread and ulcerate until much of the surface of the fish is affected. While severely affected fish die prematurely, lightly affected ones can probably spawn successfully. Whether UDN is actually confined to migratory salmonids seems to be a matter of opinion. Certainly both brown and rainbow trout can be found with a disease having all the characteristics of UDN, but the actual cause of the disease remains uncertain.

For those interested, a paper by R. J. Roberts and B. J. Hill has been published, in vol 8 (1976) of the *Journal of Fish Biology*, which strongly suggests that the disease in brown trout is the same as the well known UDN of salmon and sea trout, and also indicating that the lesions healed very frequently in brown trout, especially when water temperatures were high.

It is often supposed to be a viral infection initially, and certainly the bacteria and fungi associated with severe lesions seem to have moved in as secondary infections after the UDN has been established.

Only some rivers and lakes seem to be affected, and movement of fish from affected to unaffected waters is currently not permitted.

6

Food and Feeding Habits

I stand knee-deep in a southern stream eagerly searching for a sign of the elusive trout. It is now one o'clock and I have scanned the river since morning to no avail. Not a fin to be seen, even with the best in polaroid glasses. All these other fishermen must have cleaned it out, or could there have been some overnight disaster with cyanide? I wildly imagine all sorts of explanations for the lack of fish. Could they all have migrated elsewhere, perhaps suddenly indwelt by an irresistible longing for the sea?

Then in solitary splendour riding the swift current like a yacht, wings held aloft, the first of the day, a medium olive floats by. I have only just begun to wonder at it when another appears, this time faintly fluttering in the glances of sunlight. Some seconds later the incredible happens. Another dun, calmly sailing on the stream surface, having emerged from secret weedbeds far upstream, has his gentle ride abruptly terminated in a neat whorl of water. Where no trout was, at least to my eyes, there has suddenly appeared from nowhere a brownie of some 1½lb, now feeding deliberately. Further up stream, the rings of water tell me that another trout is busy. As I lengthen my line and nervously consider how to cover the first hungry fish with my fly I ponder for an instant, as a thousand fishermen before me, at the marvel of the feeding habits of *Salmo trutta*. Did my trout know that a hatch of duns was due at one o'clock precisely, or was he keeping a sharp eye open under some cunning camouflage of trailing weed?

The food and feeding habits of trout and grayling constitute a fascinating topic still only partially understood and leaving plenty of scope for discussion and conjecture over future pipefuls of tobacco. What I plan to do in this and the following chapter, is to commence by discussing the food items themselves, variable as they are at different times of the year and in different waters, and then to proceed to comment on how these food items are actually acquired by the fish and how feeding behaviour is best understood.

THE FOOD OF TROUT AND GRAYLING

Let me say at the outset to this section that I am not one of those who believes that a great knowledge of entomology or invertebrate biology is essential to successful game fishing in any waters. I present this discussion of the food of trout and grayling more because it may, I hope, help to enhance the enjoyment of fishing for some, or partially satisfy the curiosity of others. As will become evident later, I am somewhat sceptical that many of our tied imitations of natural insects are regularly taken by fish because of a precise resemblance to one species which they are at that time seeking as food.

I must also stress that I am in no way trying to compete with a number of excellent books written for fishermen about natural and artificial flies. Such classic books as Harris's *An Angler's Entomology*, Goddard's *Trout Flies of Stillwater* and *Trout Fly Recognition* and Jacques's *Fisherman's Fly* are too good to be easily improved on. Rather, what I am aiming to achieve is a brief outline of the main food objects of game fishes in a variety of waters, with rather more emphasis on when fish do actually exploit these food sources. Some recent information has appeared in the biological literature on this topic, which has not perhaps percolated through to the anglers who may well be interested in it.

A great variety of different items of food may occasionally find their way into the stomachs of trout and grayling. I well remember one beautiful day in late May having the greatest difficulty in bringing a response from a freely rising trout only twenty yards below a glorious hawthorn tree. When at last I rose and hooked the fish and brought it to the net, what do you think its stomach was stuffed with? Hawthorn petals! That trout had been rising steadily to a hatch (or rather a fall) of hawthorn petals, and apparently enjoying the experience. But we need only concern ourselves with the common food items and can safely ignore the gastronomic specialities of highly individualistic fish or very specialised situations. Many are the stories of giant trout which have waxed exceeding large in mill lades into which run the drains of a butcher's shop. One's imagination takes flight at the thought of a fish feeding vigorously on chopped mince or the occasional loin chop.

But, back to the realms of reality. First a list of the top twenty items of food in fresh water of trout and grayling. Some of these are groups of species; where different stages in the life history of the same group or individual organism involve widely different feeding behaviour, I have listed them separately.

Since numbers 1, 2, 3, 4, 10, 13, and 17 are either bottom living organisms or are not susceptible to satisfactory imitation by the fisherman, it will be clear that the problem of catching

THE TOP TWENTY

1. Snails – *Mollusca*
2. Shrimps – *Gammarus*
3. Water fleas – *Daphnia*
4. Worms – *Oligochaetes*
5. Beetles – *Coleoptera*
6. Bugs – *Hemiptera*
7. 'Mayfly' larvae – *Ephemeroptera*
8. 'Mayfly' duns – *Ephemeroptera*
9. 'Mayfly' spinners – *Ephemeroptera*
10. Midge larvae – *Chironomids*
11. Midge pupae – *Chironomids*
12. Midge adults – *Chironomids* (buzzers)
13. Caddis fly larvae and pupae – *Trichoptera*
14. Caddis fly adults – *Trichoptera* (sedges)
15. Hawthorn fly adults – *Diptera-Bibio* (black gnats)
16. Fish – sticklebacks, minnows, and other fry
17. Stonefly nymphs – *Plecoptera*
18. Simulium larvae – *Diptera* (reed smuts)
19. Simulium adults
20. Blown food – greenfly, ants, craneflies and spiders

trout and grayling by imitating natural food is a fairly limited exercise. The complications arise when we begin to analyse the many different types and species involved in numbers 8, 9, and 20. It must also be stressed that while some of these food items are common and highly significant as fish food in some localities, they may be entirely absent from others. For example, Daphnia are only common in some stillwaters at very restricted times of the year, but when they are present, beware – the trout may be feeding on nothing else!

I would now wish to draw my readers' attention to the interesting data on *Tables 6.1* and *6.2*. You will notice that separate tables have been drawn up for the seasonal importance of food for grayling in river conditions and trout in lake conditions. Trout in rivers will have a seasonal diet very roughly similar to that indicated for grayling. Many variants to these categories exist, but intelligence and observation should enable the angler to determine from the tables what he is likely to encounter in different places and at different times. The tables are expressed in terms of the top twenty only and groups are taken as units.

Some notes on the data of trout and grayling diets

It is important to stress that over-generalisation and dogma is easiest in complex and poorly understood topics, and this is one of them. Many fishermen have strong opinions on fish diet based on many careful autopsies on fish after capture. What they tend to forget is that these are only the fish which have been caught and may be quite unrepresentative of the others uncaught. Indeed, they may well have been caught because they were taking an unusual diet. Fishermen probably take fish rather rarely which are heavily occupied in feeding on Daphnia, caddis fly larvae, snails, or even fish fry.

Again, it is crucial to realise that fish of different sizes may have very different diets in the same water. While small fish may be taking Daphnia to the exclusion of all else, larger fish may be feeding on sticklebacks or midge pupae.

Finally a word about what the figures mean. Much work on

	J F	M	A	M	J	J	A	S	O	N	D
1 Snail	No data	19	8	19	28	16	20	22	3	19	31
2 Shrimp	″	30	19	18	7	21	15	20	61	26	34
3 Daphnia	″										
4 Worms	″										
5 Beetles	″	14	10	2	6	0	1	2	4	6	2
6 Bugs	″	0	0	0	1	0	2	1	0	3	0
7 "Mayfly" larvae	″	12	1	9	1	2	2	13	4	14	2
8 "Mayfly" duns	″	1	2	3	4	2	2	3	3	5	0
9 "Mayfly" spinners	″										
10 Midge larvae	″	4	44	32	41	24	23	16	5	9	6
11 Midge pupae	″										
12 Midge adults	″										
13 Caddis larvae + pupae	″	3	2	7	2	4	8	8	4	12	10
14 Caddis adults	″										
15 Bibio	″										
16 Fish	″										
17 Stonefly nymphs	″	0	1	0	0	1	1	0	1	0	1
18 Simulium nymphs	″	11	3	2	4	24	14	11	2	2	3
19 Simulium adults	″	0	0	0	0	1	1	0	0	0	0
20 Blown surface food	″	0	3	1	4	5	4	2	2	1	1
21 Other unlisted	″	6	7	7	2	0	7	6	11	3	10

Table 6.1

Percentage composition of grayling stomachs in different months. Figures are expressed as percentage numbers of individual organisms. Since the volume of different organisms varies greatly, the contribution of these food items to the grayling diet varies, being high for shrimp for example, and low for midge larvae. Some food items are not listed and unfortunately no data are available for the months of January and February. (Data based largely on Singh 'Some contributions to the Biology of the Grayling' M.Sc. Thesis, but modified by other data and observations.)

		J	F	M	A	M	J	J	A	S	O	N	D
1	Snail	19	2	20	16	26	0	0	0	8	10	50	25
2	Shrimp												
3	Daphnia	0	0	0	0	0	8	98	0	0	0	0	0
4	Worms												
5	Beetles	0	0	1	2	2	0	0	0	1	1	0	0
6	Bugs	0	0	0	1	4	0	0	0	15	57	0	0
7	"Mayfly" larvae	16	37	16	6	2	0	0	0	0	1	1	1
8	"Mayfly" duns												
9	"Mayfly" spinners												
10	Midge larvae	17	20	22	15	20	1	0	1	0	1	7	13
11	Midge pupae	0	0	0	15	14	84	1	93	54	0	0	0
12	Midge adults												
13	Caddis larvae + pupae	33	30	24	23	14	2	0	0	12	7	20	47
14	Caddis adults												
15	Bibio adults	0	0	0	0	3	0	0	0	0	0	0	0
16	Fish	0	0	0	0	0	1	0	4	6	6	6	0
17	Stonefly nymphs												
18	Simulium nymphs												
19	Simulium adults												
20	Blown surface food	0	0	2	15	11	4	1	2	6	8	0	0
21	Other unlisted	15	11	15	7	4	0	0	1	8	0	6	15

Table 6.2

Percentage composition of trout stomachs in different months, expressed as percentage numbers of individual organisms. As with Table 6.1 the actual volume of these organisms varies greatly and thus their comparative contribution to the diet of the trout is very different to that suggested by the table. These figures can only be taken as a rough indication of what stillwater trout eat. The lakes studied here had a negligible shrimp population. If this had been high, so too would the shrimp contribution be in the trout diet. Note also the concentration of feeding effort on Daphnia in July, Midge pupae in August, and small fish in September to November. These features of the diet vary from one water to another but are characteristic of many. The data are compiled from various papers in the *Journal of Fish Biology* and elsewhere, but I am guilty of fudging the figures to make the data from individual papers more generally applicable. I have thus had to sacrifice strict scientific accuracy in order to avoid misleading my less academic readers. Some authors have made similar studies to these but have expressed their results in percentage volume or weight of the diet. Sadly, I have had to ignore these interesting studies since they could not be transformed into organism numbers.

fish diet is difficult to compare or interpret because different parameters are measured. If the numbers of food items are scored, then 10 000 water fleas may not equal one small frog in terms of volume or food significance. On the other hand, even if it takes 50 midge pupae to equal the bulk of one caddis fly larvae, there is still a 50 to 1 ratio of food-taking assuming that each pupa is individually taken. I have chosen to express all tables and figures as percentages on a volume basis. But no one approach is ideal.

I will discuss more fully in the following text the seasonal variations of the individual species listed under 8, 9, and 20. Some of the data is incomplete, especially that for grayling, where no figures are available for the crucial months of December, January and February. From my own observations of grayling food and stomachs, these months are not unlike March and November, and the following table based on year-round data of grayling food provides a simplified view.

Composition of grayling food by percentage volume

Midge larvae	11%
Gammarus	20%
Snail	18%
Simulium larvae	12%
'Mayfly' nymphs	15%
Trichoptera larvae	8%
The rest	16%

The grayling is clearly a fish which feeds primarily on or near the river bottom on shrimp, snails and fly larvae. By bulk, most grayling are heavily dependent on our old friend the freshwater shrimp *Gammarus*, and obviously any dry fly feeding by grayling is a matter of providing the dessert to a substantial main course of shrimp. I think this menu also implies that bait fishing with artificial representatives of shrimp might prove very successful. Quite probably many heavily hackled wet fly patterns may be taken by grayling in mistake for shrimp and should be fished for optimum effect as near to the bottom as possible. At certain seasons of the year, especially October and November, grayling do feed quite actively on surface fly, especially Ephemeropteran duns, and at this time provide an interesting challenge to the dry fly man. They can be very fastidious in their choice of fly and in clear waters are every bit as gut shy as the most discriminating of trout. Anyone who thinks dry fly fishing for grayling is easy, has never fished in any but coloured or very rough water.

Composition of trout food by percentage volume

	In an average lake with low Gammarus population	*In an average river*
	%	%
Trichoptera larvae	27	16
Ephemeroptera larvae	5	11
Chironomid pupae	11	8
Gammarus	0.01	25
Daphnia	1.2	—
Beetles	0.6	1
Fish	27	0.5
Snails	8	0.5
Surface flies	10	25
Others	10	10

These percentages are only crude approximations, for each lake or river is unique and indeed each section, pool or bay will have its own special characteristics and food-chain balance. But let me try to catalogue some general conclusions about trout and grayling food items and their importance for the fisherman.

Oligochaetes Neither worms nor maggots feature normally as an important part of the diet of trout or grayling. Both fish will take some worms from lake or river bottoms but they will be encountered only occasionally in the food search.

Gammarus In many rivers and some lakes, the freshwater shrimp is the most important item of trout and grayling food. At certain times and places this one organism may provide 50 per cent of the diet of either fish.

Daphnia The water flea, is found almost exclusively in lakes and there is normally a fantastic population explosion to produce a bloom of Daphnia in July. At such times that may constitute over 90 per cent of the food of some trout by bulk! So be warned, lake fishing in July can be a waste of time apart perhaps from a very brief evening rise to surface fly. Of course, July is normally a difficult time for fly fishing even on rivers.

Chironomid pupae Chironomids are small non-biting midges, often called buzzers, and most species spend their larval stages in water, especially in mud. There they finally pupate, but before hatching the pupa wriggles its way to the water surface, where it hatches into the adult. Perhaps the single most important development in stillwater fly fishing of recent years has been a growing appreciation of the importance of the pupae of these midges in the trout diet – see *The Pursuit of Stillwater Trout* by Bryan Clarke.

But this development must be viewed with mixed emotion, for whilst it may lead to good sport and the satisfactory hooking and catching of many trout, the rise to fame of the Chironomid pupa is not just a change in the awareness of the angler. In all probability it also betokens a change in many of our lakes, with bottom silt replacing sand and gravel, and consequently Chironomids replacing Ephemeropterans. Such changes are almost certainly induced largely by the process of eutrophication, that is, reduction in oxygen, and high nitrogen content brought about by the persistent seepage of nitrogenous fertiliser into the lake. As I comment elsewhere, there is ample evidence that even large bodies of water such as Chew and Blagdon are affected by this malaise, as also in Loch Leven in Scotland. Under eutrophic conditions the trout will probably feed less on hatching fly, rather more on Daphnia, fish fry, and snails. When they do rise, it will frequently be to take the Chironomid pupa *in* the surface film rather than insects *on* the water surface.

Chironomid pupae constitute an average 10 per cent of the diet of lake trout and in June that figure may at times rise to 80 per cent in some waters. So there is clearly plenty of scope for the use of midge pupae imitations fished on or below the surface film.

I have stressed the Chironomid pupae chiefly because the larvae are mud-dwelling and the adults largely terrestrial, so neither are anywhere near as important to the angler as the pupa.

Trichoptera larvae Not until I came to do some background reading for this chapter did I realise the importance of the caddis fly larva as a food item for trout and grayling, but particularly the former. Between 15 and 30 per cent of the diet (by bulk) of trout may be made up of these creatures. But I see no easy way of our using such knowledge to engineer the capture of these fish. It just seems to be an interesting observation.

Ephemeropteran larvae We have always known, on the other hand, that nymphs (larvae) of the mayfly group were highly important constituents of diet for riverine trout and grayling. 5 to 15 per cent (by bulk) seems to be the figure, and clearly their imitation provides plenty of scope for the wet fly man.

Fish Arguments have raged for many years in the angling press over the question of whether lake trout regularly eat small fish. The results of careful scientific assays of stomach contents are indisputable. In many lakes, fish fry and small fish species may be a very important food item, varying between 5 and 35 per cent of the food material by bulk. Most of these fish are sticklebacks, but in some lakes and reservoirs minnows, perch fry and roach fry are important, especially when these species shoal in late May and June.

Surface flies In this one category are wrapped up all the many treasured items of fish food which induce the surface rise. They include 'mayfly' type duns and spinners, sedges, midges, occasional Simulium and stoneflies, and blown terrestrial insects such as ants, crane flies, spiders and aphids. Surface flies rarely make up more than 10 per cent of the trout or grayling diet, even less where bottom feeding is rich or surface feeding poor. But, as a generalisation, small and very large trout take few surface items in stillwater fisheries, while medium sized fish may take them very actively. In stillwaters with poor bottom feeding, such as peaty lochs, surface flies, especially blown terrestrial insects, may make up the vast majority of trout food. In rivers it is more difficult to generalise, but something like a tenth of a trout's food is likely to be surface, less for grayling.

A general conclusion

A general conclusion is that, while the diet of both trout and grayling is mixed, that of the grayling is probably much more constant than that of the trout. Not only is the menu of the trout rather varied even on the basis of our top twenty, but at certain times many fish may be working one food item to the near exclusion of all else.

A more detailed description of the top twenty

Snails (*Mollusca*)

Freshwater snails are known to the taxonomist as Gastropod Molluscs. The word gastropod means 'gutfoot', implying that the muscular 'foot' on which it moves also contains part of the digestive system. Many species of mollusc live in fresh water and sometimes their numbers can be very high. I have selected four species for special mention because they are common and represent distinct types. It is likely that, if both rivers and lakes are considered, at least thirty different species of snail will contribute to the diet of trout and grayling, but some of these are rare or confined to very specialised localities. On the other hand, the abundance of some species of snail may surprise anglers. One little snail called *Hydrobia* which only turned up in this country in the late 1860's has become very common with densities of many thousands per square yard.

With all this delectable food around, it is little wonder that trout and grayling feed so heavily on snail and it is not uncommon to find lake trout with their stomachs full of snail shells.

Limnaea is a genus of very common snails, often occurring in ponds and weedy lakes. They have a tendency to congregate at the edges of ponds and may leave the water on occasions to browse on the weedy margins. The largest have thick shells and are rarely if ever eaten by fish, but small specimens are readily eaten, especially since they are comparatively soft-shelled and presumably readily broken by the fish.

Rams-horn snails are, like the larger *Limnaea*, collected by small boys with jam jars and nets. The small rams-horns are in the genus known as *Planorbis* and are avidly collected by trout from off the stems of water plants on which they graze. Whilst *Limnaea* and *Planorbis* are commonest in lakes, the valve snails are typical of riverine habitats. The shells of these snails are somewhat flattened in shape and are beloved of caddis fly larvae for the construction of their incredible tube-shaped dwellings. Valve snails are in the genus *Valvata*.

Our last gastropod snail is distinct from the others since it is a small limpet. Freshwater limpets occur in both lakes and rivers and since each has a different generic name I will not trouble to introduce them.

One other mollusc of both rivers and stillwaters deserves mention although it is not a gastropod but a small two-shelled bivalve mollusc. This is the tiny freshwater pea mussel, *Pisidium*. Lake trout often gorge on pea mussels, and they are normally very abundant at all depths in lakes with somewhat muddy bottoms. It is likely that trout take Chironomid larvae and pea mussels from mud much as carp do, by sucking up and blowing out mouthfuls of mud. I have seen trout doing just this in a shallow stretch of mud by the lakeside and suspect that they were harvesting molluscs. Pea mussels of this and other genera are also common in rivers, especially in fine gravel, and once again the trout and grayling are often to be seen working the gravel in search of these and other small molluscs.

Shrimps (*Gammarus*)

The freshwater shrimp, *Gammarus*, is a small crustacean creature, some ½ inch long when full grown, and flattened sideways. As already indicated, they are of the greatest importance as food items for both grayling and trout. It is probable that the fish often seek them out by shifting the stones on the river or lake bed with their snouts or tails. Freshwater shrimps are close relatives of the familiar sand hoppers and indeed share the same generic name. Our commonest species is *Gammarus pulex* and, although by no means confined to them, is found most abundantly in limestone lakes and streams. No doubt this abundance in alkali waters is explained by the requirement for calcium carbonate for construction of the shrimps' outer shell. This principle applies also to the mollusca of course, and is particularly evident in the case of *Astacus*, the freshwater crayfish, which is confined to very chalky waters, presumably by its high calcium requirement. Most good fishery managers know how important *Gammarus* is to them and do all in their power to encourage its success, even to the extent of introducing it to new lakes and gravel pits if not already present.

Gammarus is possessed of a broad pouch and in late spring you may find individuals with numerous tiny young shrimps in their pouches. The pink flesh of many trout is derived from their intake of carotene (a pigment which takes its name from carrots which contain it), which is present in both snails and shrimps. Trout farmers now sometimes add carotene to trout food in order to induce the desirable pink colour.

Water fleas (*Daphnia*)

Like *Gammarus*, water fleas are crustaceans, and are enclosed in a minute shell. Many different kinds are known but none better than *Daphnia*. In late July their numbers often reach astonishing proportions in stillwaters and they are essential food for the fish fry which are then evident. Large trout seem to ignore *Daphnia* until their numbers reach certain critical

Plate I. The rainbow trout (above) and the grayling. The trout depicted here is in breeding colours and therefore darker and more deeply coloured than mid-season rainbow trout caught during the months of April to October.

Plate 2. The fish's window. This photograph was taken with a fish eye lens camera placed about 9 inches below the surface of the river Itchen. Notice the clarity with which the detail of fly and leader on the surface are seen, and also the figures on the bank. The large dark figure nearest to the centre of the photograph is the photographer. I am greatly indebted to Miss Jenny Mallinson and Mr Ken Collins of the Southampton University Sub Aqua Club for this interesting photograph.

Plate 3. A male *Chironomid* midge, highly magnified. This insect and its larvae and pupae is perhaps the single most important insect food of trout in present day fisheries.

Plate 4. A ferox trout, with two normal trout, taken from Loch Veyatie, Sutherland, Scotland. The ferox trout is a hen fish of at least 15 years of age, 65.5 cms (approx. 24 inches) long and weighing 3.2 kg. (approx. 7 lbs). Ferox brown trout in this and other waters feed substantially on char (*Salvelinus alpinus*). Details of this interesting strain of brown trout are to be found in a paper by R. N. Campbell published in the *Journal of Fish Biology* (1979) volume 14.

Plate 5. A fine brown trout from the river Test, weighing just over 3 lbs, held by the author's son Gavin (himself a budding fisherman).

Plate 6. A stretch of the Wiltshire Avon in November. Such pools as this present exciting grayling fishing for both the fly fisherman and the 'long trotter' using worm or maggot baits.

Plate 7. Stock rainbow trout in a North American lake. Such dense concentrations of large fish would not normally occur in natural conditions.

Plate 8. These photographs, taken from below the water surface using an underwater camera, show a live Olive Dun (*Baetis* species) above, and a dry winged artificial Greenwell's Glory, a popular artificial imitation of the Olive Dun, below. The artificial is tied on a no. 14 hook, dressed with floatant oil, and attached to a 5x nylon leader. Notice that, against the bright background of sky, both objects appear largely in silhouette, and their colour is only vaguely detectable. We can conclude that the colour of artificial dry flies is probably not of paramount importance as compared to the general size and shape of the fly. These photographs were taken with the camera and fly in line vertically. From any other angle (and the feeding fish will see flies from many angles) the hook of the artificial is much more evident than this picture suggests.

density. The trout then take to feeding on them much as basking sharks exploit the plankton in the sea, that is, by swimming along with their mouths open. Of course, basking sharks are specially adapted to sieve the small plankton with special gill rakers, but trout must simply close up their gill lamellae sufficiently to let the water out but keep the fleas in. When the trout in your favourite lake are feeding on *Daphnia*, pack up and find a pleasant local hostelry. You will be better occupied!

Worms (*Oligochaetes*)

Worms come in many kinds, but the sorts eaten by game fish or used as bait in their pursuit, are termed Oligochaetes. Some of these are small worms living in mud, others are the larger earthworms with which we are all familiar. We will return in Chapter 8 to a fuller discussion about the merits of worms as bait, but need only briefly say here that neither trout nor grayling normally eat worms in large numbers, yet hungrily devour them when offered. Quite possibly much of the feeding behaviour of fish is instinctive rather than learned, and so, even if a young fish has never encountered a worm before or savoured its gastronomic delights, it instinctively knows a good thing when it sees one. Did you know of the recent culinary exercise in England which offered a reward for the best worm recipe? Many entries were attracted, too! But this apart, many species of Oligochaete are aquatic, not only the little red *Tubifex*, beloved as fish food by aquarists, which can be seen girating its body from tubes in silted stretches of the river, but also a species called *Caetogaster* which closely resembles a normal earthworm. These are probably the worms most often found and eaten by trout and grayling in flood condition.

Beetles (*Coleoptera*)

Beetles belong to the order of insects called the Coleoptera and their importance as a constituent of fish diet varies greatly from one water to another. Small water beetles, living below the surface, are very abundant in some lakes and are taken readily by the resident trout. But water beetles are infrequent in the rivers beloved by trout and grayling. Here their place is taken by terrestrial beetles which are occasionally found on the water surface, especially in water which is thickly overgrown by plants and trees. These land-based beetles are often eaten, and I have seen trout eating the soft-bodied soldier beetles which are left alone by birds because of their distasteful contents. Perhaps the situation where beetles are most important as trout food is in small land-locked mountain lakes, where bottom feeding is poor and the fish are very dependent on blown insects on the surface. Small beetles from the grasses and heather are then eaten readily and commonly found in trout stomachs.

Bugs (*Hemiptera*)

To the biologist bugs are a special order of insects; the Hemiptera. They include many familiar land insects and a few aquatic ones. The only bugs which make much contribution to game fish diet are the water-boatmen, an often abundant insect in weedy lakes. Amongst the commonest small water-boatmen are some which belong to the genus *Corixa*, and most fishermen now refer to water-boatmen as corixids (to the naturalist the true water-boatmen is a related insect which swims on its back – *Notonecta* by name). *Corixa* is a brown-backed, white-bellied, beetle-like insect, with an erratic swimming technique and a need for frequent return to the surface for air (as have also the water beetles). Although some grayling flies are referred to as 'bugs', in fact *Corixa* are very infrequent in fast streams and are probably never encountered by grayling. Recently flooded gravel pits with a high weed content are often teeming with small *Corixa* and in these situations imitations of the insect, fished slow and fairly deep, can be very successful.

'Mayfly' larvae (*Ephemeroptera*)

These insects comprise an order of four-winged flies of which the mayfly is the most famous. The larvae are aquatic, living for the most part on water plants in lakes and rivers, and many are highly active swimmers. These larvae are known as nymphs, and such men as G. E. M. Skues and Oliver Kite have pioneered the capture of trout by carefully presented artificial nymphs, fished upstream. It is probable that the wet flies used for generations in the rough upland streams of our country are, in many cases, taken by fish in mistake for these nymphs. Some are long and slender, some short and tubby; most are greenish to brown in colour. Almost all have three (sometimes two) rather prominent tails at the hind end and small feathery gills along the abdomen, which gives them a somewhat ragged appearance. Some nymphs, such as those of the large 'Green Drake' mayfly *Ephemera damica*, are burrowing and probably rarely found by fish, but other species regularly crawl and swim, and form an important constituent of trout and grayling food.

Since it is probable that swimming nymphs are more frequently eaten by game fish than any others, we should take more careful note of the appearance and habits of these species. Two which are fairly representative are the nymphs of the Lake Olive fly, *Cloëon simile*, which is common in lakes, and of the Large Dark Olive, *Baetis rhodani*, which is confined to rivers. Both these nymphs are slim elongated agile creatures with dark head and thorax, slightly yellowish legs and abdomen, and long tails. The former nymph is the smaller of the two, being about 15mm in length, while the *Baetis* nymph is about 20mm, almost one inch. Both of these insect larvae have a darting jerky manner of swimming. If you have ever tried to catch shrimps in a rock pool by the seaside you will remember the sudden movement. Completely still one moment, six inches away the next. These nymphs move rather like that, surprisingly swiftly for so delicate a creature, but of course their swimming is normally confined to fairly smooth water. Hardly for them the maelstrom of the main current, but rather, shortish swims from one frond of crowfoot to the next or, greatly daring, one weedbed to another. Nymphs of some species confine their movements to crawling, others move through the water in rapid darts, while yet others are adept swimmers with a more steady progression through the water.

When fishing artificial nymphs either upstream or down, I suppose the trick is to sink the thing and then to impart to it some of these jerky movements. I do not find it at all easy, but Oliver Kite seemed to have little difficulty in imparting authentic movement to his well sunken nymphs. His experience was that the fish almost invariably took when the nymph was moved in this way.

For any of my readers whose fascination with the ways and wiles of nymphs is not yet satisfied, I can recommend Harris's *An Angler's Entomology* for a much more detailed account.

'Mayfly' duns (*Ephemeroptera*)

One of the curiosities of the 'Mayfly' order is that the nymph hatches into a 'fly' which is not itself the final form of the insect. The first 'fly', the subimago of the biologist, is called a dun by the angler, and it is a slightly heavier version of the final insect. It is these duns which we all watch with fascination as they sit on the water surface, wings aloft, sailing with the current like miniature galleons. The actual emergence of the dun from the last nymphal stage occurs at the surface, and is remarkably rapid. Duns are poor fliers and cannot make headway against even a gentle breeze, but seek waterside vegetation in sheltered bays where they may undergo their last moult to yield the final 'fly' – the imago to the biologist; spinner to the fisherman.

Of spinners more anon. For the moment let us take a longer look at the duns. Many dry flies, both winged and unwinged, are made as copies of Ephemeropteran duns. We should note, as we examine the natural insect and its copy, that a dun sits on the water, legs widely spread, wings upright but sometimes slightly separated, body held off the surface film and the abdomen curved up away from the water with the tail streamers well up. The time spent by duns on the water surface depends on temperature and sunlight. On cool cloudy days the duns may travel for quite long distances on rivers, or sit out on lake surfaces for say ten minutes before flying. But on warm sunny days they may fly almost immediately after hatching, perhaps because the wings have dried quickly and the flight muscles have warmed up.

Table 6.3 gives brief details of ten common duns of major importance to the game fisherman. We can take comfort from the fact that in most situations only a few of these ten species are likely to be encountered, e.g. Lake Olives, Small Spurwings, Mayfly and Caenis on lakes and reservoirs; Claret Duns and March Browns on northern streams and burns, and Blue Winged Olives, Iron Blues, and Small Spurwings when fishing dry fly for autumn grayling.

As far as imitative patterns are concerned I am very doubtful about the usefulness of carrying supposed copies of even the majority of these flies. I personally find that a range of sizes of Greenwell's Glory, together with some small dark Iron Blue type flies, some small badger hackled ones for *Caenis*, a few Mayfly and March Brown imitations, and some really dark dun hackled flies for Claret Dun hatches in the north, covers most eventualities from chalk streams to Highland lochans. My suspicion is that this range of patterns could be further reduced without noticeable effect on the annual catch statistics.

'Mayfly' spinners (*Ephemeroptera*)

When a 'mayfly' dun moults it emerges as an adult spinner. These flies, in contrast to the dull heavy wings of the duns, have clear shimmering wings, and with them they fly quite strongly with a characteristic flapping flight. Much of their time is spent in courtship flights, often overland and generally in large communal clouds of flies. After mating, the females return to the water to lay eggs, after which they fall on the water surface as dead or dying flies. Spinners fall on the water with wings outstretched in the 'spent' position and so are flat on the surface film and much more difficult to detect than the duns. Fish often feed on small spinners by tiny sipping rises which are sometimes scarcely detectable.

Although the spinners of many species lay their eggs by shedding them in flight, others descend on to the water surface to do so. Indeed, the female spinners of some species such as the Large Dark Olive and the Iron Blue actually crawl down below the surface and lay their eggs subaquatically.

In general the imitative patterns for spinners are best used in an unwinged hackled form, and I favour lightly hackled badger or pale blue hackles for spinners with some variation in the colour of the body. Fish dedicated to the consumption of spinners can be very resistant to any form of artificial fly, no matter how skilfully devised and delicately presented.

Midge larvae (*Chironomids*)

Chironomids, which are non-biting midges, and somewhat larger than the biting varieties, appear to be the fly fisherman's discovery of the 1970's. This is not simply because of the current emphasis on stillwaters, where admittedly these flies have always been common, but probably also because the midge population has increased and the 'mayfly' have regressed, as lakes and reservoirs have developed the 'eutrophic' disease (see discussion on page 80).

The larvae of most of these flies live in the mud at the bottom of lakes and ponds, and are long slightly worm-like creatures. Two general colours occur, red and green, the former being commonest in poorly oxygenated waters (they are red because of the presence of abundant haemoglobin necessary for survival in these conditions). Trout probably harvest Chironomid larvae from mud in lakes and slow rivers, but there is probably little that we can hope to gain by imitating these larvae. It is the next stage in the midge life history which gives the angler some scope for adding to his basket of fish.

Midge pupae (*Chironomids*)

The midge larvae pupate in the mud and, after a period of rest, the pupa sets off for the surface film where it will hatch into the

Common Names	Latin Names	Season	Imitative Fly Patterns	Localities
Blue Winged Olive	*Ephemerella ignita*	June–December	Orange Quill and Sherry Spinner	Most fast streams
Claret Dun	*Leptophlebia vespertina*	May and June		Acid lochs and streams
Large Dark Olive	*Baetis rhodani*	Spring and autumn	Blue Dun and Red Spinner	Most rivers
Iron Blue	*Baetis pumilis*	April–November		Medium and fast rivers in most of Britain
Small Spurwing (pale watery)	*Controptilum lateolum*	May–November	Little Marryat	Lakes and rivers in most of Britain, but especially limestone rivers
Medium Olive	*Baetis vernus*	April–September	Greenwell's Glory	Chiefly chalk streams
Lake Olive	*Cloëon simile*	April–September		Sheltered bays of many lakes
Mayfly (Green Drake)	*Ephemera danica*	May and June	Spent Gnat (spinner)	Lakes and rivers, especially alkaline. Very uneven distribution
March Brown	*Rhithrogena laarupi*	March and April		Welsh, northern England and Scottish rivers
Caenis (Angler's curse)	*Caenis* species	June–August (morning and evening)		Several species on both lakes and rivers in most of Britain

Table 6.3 A table showing characteristics of some common Ephemeroptera.

adult fly. It can be a long journey. Midge larvae are common in mud twenty feet down in lakes and reservoirs and the pupae have to wriggle their lonely way up through twenty feet of inhospitable water to reach the surface. In any lake with a good stock of trout it must be a dangerous journey, for trout take these pupae very avidly. Fortunately for us, the anglers, the pupae rise quite quickly through the water but hang for a short time just in or below the surface film before hatching. This is when the trout seem to specialise in their collection and when the artful fisherman can hope to skilfully introduce his mocked-up copy. Midges hatch more evenly and regularly than Ephemeropterans, especially in the evening, and so the midge pupa patterns are always a sound choice on stillwaters.

Midge adults [buzzers] (*Chironomids*)

Adult flies of these species are very easily recognised by their long legs, single pair of wings and elaborate shaggy antennae (although often only the males sport these). These adult midges, or buzzers as the angler calls them, are actually not a major feature of trout diet since they tend to leave the water after hatching and spend most of their life on land. But considerable falls of spent midges sometimes appear on the surface of lakes and the trout will then readily take them.

Caddis fly larvae and pupae (*Trichoptera*)

Caddis flies are the sedges of the angler and any of us who cannot remember with delight the first schoolboy wonderment at discovering a larval caddis fly beneath a stone, has suffered a deprived boyhood. These extraordinary creatures, pale naked grubs when withdrawn from their cases, build elaborate and attractive homes for themselves from many of the materials available on the river bed – sand grains, pieces of plant material, or empty mollusc shells. Each tube is marvellously executed to yield a work of art – not quite dry-stone dyking, since the pieces of material or grains of sand are stuck together on the inside by a sticky silk exuded by the larva – but an intricately integrated tube of the appropriate material. Tubes of different materials are the products of different caddis fly species, so each species is itself a specialist craftsman in some particular medium.

The caddis fly larva, though soft and unprotected for most of its length (withdrawn from the tube that is) is quite strongly armoured at the head end by a tough head and thorax and three pairs of stout walking legs. Nevertheless, when danger threatens the entire larva withdraws into its tube. These larvae, although camouflaged and protected by their tube cases, must fall easy prey to carnivorous fish who no doubt eat them, cases and all. When a caddis larva ventures over the stream or lake bed, therefore, it does so at great risk to its survival, and vast numbers are eaten by trout and grayling. As with the Chironomid larva in the mud, there is no obvious way in which the astute angler can turn the fondness of grayling and trout for caddis larvae to good account in terms of his catch. Of course, caddis larvae make excellent bait and as a village lad I collected caddis grubs in my jam jar in order to use them on hooks; many a small trout and minnow lost his freedom because of his great liking for caddis grubs. I must try using them for winter grayling, since most species do not pupate until the spring. (I must admit that the prospect of searching for caddis grubs in the icy waters of a November river daunts me somewhat!)

When the caddis larva turns into a pupa it does so within the case, remaining as a pupa for some weeks before its final metamorphosis. When that time comes it bites through any constricting parts of the case and then crawls or swims somewhat uneasily to the surface. This journey of the sedge pupa is, like that of its Chironomid cousin, extremely hazardous, and many are eaten by fish. Although they are less emphatic in their hatches than some Ephemeroptera, hatches do occur quite dramatically with many pupae moving to the surface for hatching more or less in synchrony. A good sedge hatch can be every bit as exciting as a trout rise to the green drake duns of the true mayfly. Often these sedge pupae choose late evening for hatching, and indeed some hatch after dark. If you hear some very thumping rises in quiet reaches of rivers or reedy corners of lakes just as the dusk is falling, then it is probably hatching sedge.

Many fishermen fish sedge pupal imitations and apparently do well on them. If I think sedge are hatching I normally fish a large fly in the hope of simulating the hatched fly, but that is just a personal preference. But I must admit that in my close-on forty years of fishing I have only rarely witnessed trout responding really convincingly to large hatches of sedge, but maybe that is just a feature of the waters I have fished. Certainly the behaviour of trout as sedges hatch at nightfall is written up by some angling writers as if it were the London Symphony Orchestra playing the climax of Wagner's 'Flying Dutchman'!

Caddis fly adults [sedges] (*Trichoptera*)

The adult sedge fly is rather a moth-like insect, with two pairs of wings. In caddis flies, however, the wings will be found to be covered with fine hairs, and not with scales as in the moths. The wings of sedges are also held in a characteristic roof-wise fashion when the insect is at rest, so that viewed from either end they slant down over each side of the body. Most sedges have brownish wings, or at least this is commonly the colour of the larger fore wings. Another easy way to pick out a caddis fly when it flutters confidingly on to your sleeve is by its long slender antennae, usually not held aloft but dipping gracefully towards the ground. In some species these antennae reach quite extraordinary proportions, especially in some of the smaller species, such as the longhorns and silverhorns beloved by anglers, and the immensely long antennae give the insect the curious appearance, when on the wing, of flying backwards. Sedge flies have no anal cerci (tails) as do mayflies. Some fishermen may confuse them with stoneflies, but these invariably have two anal cerci. Their closest 'mimic' is the alder fly, but that insect has much more emphatic wing veination and little true wing colour. Its antennae are also less fine and attenuated.

It is difficult to generalise about the importance of adult

Trichoptera as items of food in the diet of trout and grayling, but since some species are of considerable local importance I will list a few. There are actually some 200 species of caddis fly found in Britain alone so the angler can be readily excused the task of working up a complete knowledge of all of them.

The Great Red Sedge (*Phryganea species*) At least two species are tied up here, and they constitute the largest Trichopterans on the British list. These insects have broad reddish-brown legs and noticeably segmented antennae, and are commonest between May and July. You may encounter these insects on many rivers and lakes and the hatching flies, which emerge mostly in the evening, have a characteristic habit of scuttling over the water surface. Trout often take the fly at this time with a strong lunging rise, and large brown dry flies worked jerkily over the surface may induce a nice trout to join your catch. My impression is that sometimes very large trout which have largely abandoned the pursuit of surface food, return to indulge themselves during hatches of these insects, although I must admit that it has never been my happy lot to hook one of them at this time.

Grey Sedge (*Hydropsyche species*) Again a few species are involved. This group is distinctive because the adults, which are robust flies with greyish-red wings, hatch during the day, unlike most other large sedge flies. They are also chiefly riverine, and since the larvae of these species are fond of fast streamy water, the adults are commonly found emerging on quiet stretches below fast runs.

Grannom (*Brachycentrus subnubilis*) This is a sedge of running water, with a very uneven distribution, being well-known as a fisherman's fly in Hampshire and also some Scottish and northern English streams. On many rivers it has a very uneven distribution. Bernard Aldrich, the keeper on the Broadlands stretch of the Test, has told me that the fly has, at least in the recent past, been confined to the part of that river below

Romsey (there is a story that it did at one time occur further up, but that it has been eliminated by overambitious weed-cutting) and that attempts are being made to introduce it further upstream. The grannom fly is a smallish sedge with slightly speckled wings, and may hatch in quite large numbers in mid-afternoon in the months of April to June.

Welshman's Button (*Sericostoma personatum*) was apparently so named by the great Halford. It is a very dark-winged sedge of lakes and rivers and also tends to hatch in daytime as well as evening. June to August are its main months of appearance.

The Caperer (*Halesus digitatus*) derives its name from the habit of the female fly, fluttering over the water as she lays her eggs. Its wings are mottled in pale brown and its evening hatches may be encountered in both rivers and lakes from August to October.

Silverhorns There are many different species of these small sedges, and many are common on both stillwaters and rivers. Silverhorn hatches can be very prolific and trout feed on both pupae and adults very vigorously. They are said to be one of the first types of fly to establish themselves in newly constructed artificial lakes.

Many other species of caddis fly are common on most lakes and rivers, but they differ little from the species or groups which I have chosen to mention. Please, dear reader, do not become one of those fishermen who attempt to use the pseudo one-upmanship of identifying passing sedges with great certainty in the hearing of fellow anglers. I usually find that those who identify flies of any kind in a loud voice and with much dogmatism commonly know little about them. Which is a pity, because their pronouncements have the effect of putting other anglers off the interesting side-line of identifying the trout's food. But only a fool or a really experienced entomologist will choose to be dogmatic about identifying sedges. In any event, I doubt if it is a matter of great moment to the trout fisherman, since most sedges are rather similar, and certainly the differences between living individuals of different sedge species are less than the very considerable discrepancies between a living specimen of one species and an artificial bunch of hook and tackle put together in its image. If you can make one plausible representation of a Caperer it will do an equally effective job when fish are after Grannom, Welshman's Buttons, or Grey Sedges. At least, that is my considered opinion – though after my little diatribe about dogmatism, I had better not be too emphatic about it!

Hawthorn fly adults [black gnats] (*Diptera-Bibio*)

These flies have many different names, the least appropriate of which is the Black Gnat. Black they may be, but any resemblance between these clumsy heavy-bodied flies and the fragile grace of the common gnat is hard to find. Almost all that they have in common is that both are Diptera, that is, they possess only one pair of wings. Their Latin generic name is *Bibio* and one of the species most familiar to anglers, and also the biggest, is *Bibio marci*, also called the St Mark's Fly. *Bibio johannis* is a similar but slightly smaller insect sometimes referred to as St John's Fly.

These *Bibio* species are not really aquatic insects at all, and are most often seen flying to and fro across grassy fields on hot days in May. When in flight they have a characteristic pose with long black legs dangling, like helicopters with clumsy undercarriages. Because of the sheer numbers which hatch, and partly because they do seem to favour waterside vegetation as a resting place, many find their way on to the water surface and are then eaten by trout. I have never been in a situation where there was any sign of selective preference for *Bibio* flies by trout, but I can imagine that Blagdon on a sultry May afternoon might present a rise to the Hawthorn fly.

Another group of flies, the Simulium or reed smuts, are sometimes referred to also as 'Black Gnats'. These are discussed on page 103.

Fish

Both grayling and trout are essentially carnivorous animals, with just an occasional trace of a vegetarian element in their diet. What therefore could be more suitable as diet for a carnivorous fish than the careful balance of suitable ingredients found in other live fish? There are, however, likely to be some natural constraints on this simple solution to the dietary problem, the most important of which must be the natural selection forces operating to maintain the species. Any species of animal that makes a practise of feeding on its own live brothers and sisters is likely to be selected against in the long run, if by no other problem than those of finding a mate. Cannibalism is always likely to be rare in Nature, and, for that very reason, behaviour patterns which involve feeding on species very similar to one's self are likely to be unfavoured and suppressed, just because of the threat of accidental cannibalism. (Of cannibal trout, more anon.)

But let us not imagine that fish are not an important part of the game fish diet. Only fishermen who fail to appreciate the unrepresentative nature of a small catch selected by the very nature of their capture, can ever argue the reverse. From all the work which has been carried out on the stomach contents of netted trout the evidence is clear. Fish are an important part of the diet (see *Fig. 6.1*).

A few species of fish contribute to this diet, depending on the locality and the season. Probably the one of most general importance is our old friend the three-spined stickleback. These are amongst the most catholic of fish species in their tolerance of water conditions, being found in many situations where water is brackish or quite highly polluted. The adult stickleback is probably rarely eaten, if for no other reason than that it is so well armoured by its spines – it is certainly not sheer size which is the difficulty, since trout are often found to have quite large frogs in their stomachs. But the dense shoals of young sticklebacks which are such a feature of reservoir shallows and quiet eddies in streams are undoubtedly preyed on heavily. Biologists

Fig. 6.1 An example of a food chain. The picture shows the remains of a rainbow trout (*Salmo gairdneri*) which has been left by an otter on the embankment of a reservoir. The trout had been feeding on the fry of roach (*Rutilus rutilus*) and had eaten a surprising number of these small fish.

believe that the shoaling behaviour of young fish, like the gregarious herding of antelope or red deer, is itself a protective device to reduce their ease of capture by predators. The argument is that the sudden explosive movement of a shoal confuses an invading predator and prevents his concentrating on the capture of a single individual. In addition, a shoal, by dint of inter-shoal communication, has the additional advantage of a thousand eyes with which to provide early warning of the approach of impending danger.

Stickleback fry can be found in dense shoals in July and August. Because trout feeding on these shoals capture the fry by a sudden dash into a shoal, I suspect that we cannot easily catch such trout on our lures, however fish-like they may be.

Although sticklebacks are the most widespread small fish eaten by trout, other species are of local importance. Thus, as recorded by Frost and Brown in *The Trout*, trout in Loch Derg feed heavily on perch fry in May and June; those in Windermere eat spawning minnows in May, and large numbers of elvers in spring as they enter the lake from the River Heren. Although roach are not a frequent inhabitant of good trout waters, the trout in Eye Brook apparently take large numbers of young roach when these fry are present in shoals.

River trout no doubt find fish capture more difficult than those in lakes, but I have not infrequently seen river trout rushing the stickleback and minnow shoals in slack eddies. In addition, salmon fry are sometimes eaten, and also bullheads and stone loach when they are present – as they are in many fast mountain streams and burns.

I have already indicated my scepticism that lures are frequently taken by trout in mistake for young fish, largely because trout taking lures rarely seem to have other fish in their stomachs, whilst some netted fish are found to have been feeding to saturation on fish fry yet rarely turn up in the angler's basket.

There is almost no evidence of grayling regularly feeding on other fish, and all I could turn up in a literature search was a report of unidentified fish scales in the guts of two individual grayling.

Now a last word about piscatorial cannibalism. The grand old men who were the established sages of my native village were inclined, when perambulating between home and pub – a favoured route lay past the river and thus my close acquaintance with these venerable souls – to narrate tales of legendary trout, always dark in hue, with massive heads and thin bellies, but of extravagant length. These fish, a race apart from the modest and shapely trout that we all knew, lay silent and sinister at the bottom of deep river holes, awaiting the fateful arrival of any other living creature – trout, water rat, or small boy (for all I knew). These unfortunates then met a sudden and silent end according to the narrative, and although I was never privileged to set eyes on one of these monsters, the holes in which they lived were pointed out to me with regularity and great conviction. Similar legends apply to any lakes in which the bottom is not everywhere visible, or rivers whose clarity is not adequate to show beyond question that no fish in excess of ¼lb inhabit them. Now there is no doubt that the introduction of the wels to this country has done something to reduce the impact of the ancient sagas of giant cannibal trout. Compared with a large wels (European cat-fish), which according to all accounts does devour water voles and small ducks (a large wels can be over 4 yards in length, which, for heaven's sake, is much longer than I can jump), a cannibal trout pales into mediocrity – a just fate for all such legends.

Cannibalism seems to be rather rare amongst adult trout and it is doubtful if many individual fish could live by that means alone, which is a pity, because some of the lakes and lochs I have fished were crying out for a few cannibal trout. They might have reduced the grossly over-stocked population of minute fish which I had paid a fat fee to catch. I should perhaps add that although adult trout are rarely cannibalistic, fish breeders tell me that trout fry are often highly predatory on smaller members of their own species, especially when kept at high density.

There does seem to be one situation, however, in which trout do regularly adopt a partially cannibalistic feeding behaviour, or at least an exclusively fishy diet. I refer to the so-called 'ferox' trout caught by trolling in some Scottish lochs. These fish seem to feed substantially or exclusively on the char which also inhabit these lochs and an interesting paper about their biology has recently appeared in the *Journal of Fish Biology*, written by R. N. Campbell (vol. 14, 1979, pages 1–29). Plate 4 is derived from this paper.

Stonefly nymphs (*Plecoptera*)

Stoneflies belong to the insect order Plecoptera and the adults have two pairs of wings and a pair of very conspicuous and characteristic tails or anal cerci. They also possess two long antennae which are much stouter than those of the caddis flies.

Stoneflies have aquatic nymphs which are quite substantial animals and certainly much larger than the nymphs of the Ephemeroptera. These nymphs crawl rather than swim and in small turbulent streams of the North are known as creepers.

Although stonefly adults and nymphs are not likely to be confused by fish or fishermen, and are eaten in quite different ways by the fish, I have chosen to discuss them together simply because neither is of really prime importance as a general food of game fish.

First the nymphs. These are one of the few genuine trout foods actually used as bait, and fishing the creeper is a very ancient fishing practice in the border streams. Indeed, the stonefly is most significant as an item of trout diet in northern and mountain streams, since in the southern rivers it is greatly overshadowed by sedges and mayflies. Creeper baits are normally fished very close to the bottom, and that is where the nymphs are customarily found in Nature. They are highly predatory larvae and eagerly devour the smaller nymphs of the Ephemeroptera.

Adult stoneflies spend much of their time on land, although some are commonly to be found on riverside vegetation. The August/September/October hatching Needle Fly, a very slim stonefly common on chalk streams, is one such species. But many other species are eagerly eaten by trout when egg laying, a practice which is carried out either by the female alighting on the surface and depositing eggs as she swims upstream, or by simply touching down briefly in flight to deposit her eggs. Some half-dozen species of stonefly are well known to upland stream fishermen, including the golden hued Yellow Sally (*Isoperla grammatica*), the Willow Fly (*Leuctra geniculata*) – which is a slender brown species with similar contour to the Needle Fly – and the two commonest species, which are both robust brown flies, the Large Stonefly (*Perla carlukiana*) and the Early Brown (*Protonemoura meyeri*).

When trout are feeding on stoneflies then large sedge fly patterns can be fished as imitations, although special tyings of Yellow Sally are widely used and well known.

Simulium adults (*Diptera*)

Simulium is a group of two-winged flies, belonging therefore to the order Diptera. This is the order to which the common house fly and blue-bottle belong, as also do the Chironomids. Simulium flies are slightly more substantial looking insects than Chironomids, with black bodies and clear wings; they are sometimes called 'reed smuts' or 'black flies'. The wings are broad by comparison with the proportions of most other flies, and the abdomen quite squat. Although of no direct import for the catching of fish, many fishermen know of another side to the character of Simulium, namely that they suck blood. Only the females bite and most commonly they attack horses and cattle, but in some areas they can be exceedingly troublesome to humans also. Perhaps for this reason they have been styled the Black Curse. Since they are considerably bigger than the true biting midges so prevalent in the Scottish West Highlands, their bite is more severe and perceptively painful.

Simulium are characteristic flies of small fast rivers and burns in the sheltered valleys of hilly upland areas. In such streams, and also in lakes and lochs adjoining such streams, Simulium flies may be present in large numbers and the spent flies may induce major rises by the resident trout. Very small black spiders or black-bodied, badger-hackled flies are then the traditional choice, but even flies tied with tiny hackles on No. 18 hooks are likely to look pretty hefty next to a Simulium, and fish feeding mainly on 'reed smuts' are notoriously difficult to deceive with the artificial.

Simulium larvae [reed smuts] (*Diptera*)

As I have mentioned, the normal habitat of Simulium is the fast rippling stream, and this is also true of the larvae, since they are to be found firmly attached to stones and weeds in quite fast currents of water. Thence the trout often take them and you may readily find small river trout which, on autopsy, have stomachs bulging with Simulium larvae. These larvae are also an important food of grayling in such streams, and since the grayling is more a fish of the turbulent water than is the trout, it is not surprising to note than Simulium larvae figure more importantly in grayling diet.

I am not sure that there is much that we can do by way of cashing-in on the addiction of small-river game fish for these larvae, especially since the larvae are themselves normally sedentary. Simulium larvae are cream or whitish insects which cling to their support by means of a tiny sucker at the anal end. At the other end, hanging free in the current, are a pair of plume-like brushes which are used in food gathering. These larvae are about ¼ inch in length when fully grown and slightly resemble thin and anaemic blowfly maggots.

Blown food

Although I am categorising all these organisms as 'blown' food, some may appear on the water surface even on still days by dint of flying over the water from adjoining land. Those of you who fish only on the prolific rivers of the chalk country may well ignore these insects, but those amongst us who trudge long miles over boulder-strewn heather moors to reach small lochans or remote burns will want to know all about them, for the fish which we seek depend very largely on them for their survival. On all but very still days it is well to remember that, by dint of being blown, these insects (and spiders) will be in particular parts of the water. If on rivers, they may be blown from certain fields or overhanging trees; on lakes and lochs they will be concentrated along the windward shore in a lightish breeze but may collect on the lee shore in a high wind. Also, as all lake fishermen know, within the main water they will often be found concentrated in the long lines of spume which appear, especially those where the windward and lee waters meet.

A great multitude of different creatures may be blown on to water surfaces from the surrounding country, but the chief ones are probably aphids (greenfly), beetles, ants, small spiders and craneflies (daddy-long-legs). Of these, beetles are probably too variable and aphids and spiders too small to bother the fisherman except in rather special situations. I have known fish in river pools to feed quite actively on greenfly when these were very abundant on overhanging limes, and in these circumstances I have taken fish on very small flies, presumably in mistake for aphids. Ants and craneflies are very commonly found on the water surface at certain times of the year. Ant colonies normally produce vast numbers of winged ants on hot days in June and July. This 'hatch' is a synchronous affair over quite a large area, so that on one day the air may be thick with flying ants, much to the discomfort of pedestrians. Even driving visibility may be limited by an extensive hatch. On such days any sheet of water will be littered with ants and the trout will take them eagerly.

Winged ants have two pairs of wings and hard shining bodies and resemble small wasps, with a very narrow waist between thorax and abdomen. They do, of course, belong to the same insect order as bees and wasps, the Hymenoptera.

Craneflies, on the other hand, are Diptera, having but a single pair of wings. On Irish loughs and some Scottish lochs they are either dapped live, or cranefly imitations are fished by dapping. Sea trout in such stillwaters appear to take them very readily. Since I have not been privileged to fish in celebrated dapping waters, this is not a technique I can discuss with any knowledge, but by all accounts it can be great fun.

7
Feeding Behaviour

Perhaps, from the point of view of angling as a sport, the single most important aspect of fish behaviour is that they do not feed all the time. Whether going in quest of tarpon, tench, or trout, fishermen the world over experience long periods when their quarry, though obviously present, display no interest in food nor anything which might be construed to resemble it. At other times, and how deeply are these etched in our angling memories, the fish feed with incredible eagerness and seem determined to have our baits, however poorly they may represent normal food and however crudely they are offered to the fish.

I have three such memories to relate. (I agree that writing a book about fish affords an author the indulgent opportunity rarely afforded to the angler – to regale an audience with his particular fishing stories. However, the reluctant reader has an advantage over the listener: he can, without offending, skip the next four paragraphs.)

My first concerns a November day after grayling. It was overcast but mild, and the fish showed little interest in surface fly. I had therefore decided to use wet fly fished downstream, and I knotted on to my leader a single weighted fly, tied in imitation of a small corixa. I stood at the head of a long straight stretch of some hundred yards of broken streamy water, uncomplicated by bushes or trees, and with an abundance of weed growing in about four feet of water. My method was to cast downstream and across and, immediately after the cast, to throw out enough slack line to permit my fly to sink and to work down between the weedbeds. My first fish came in a couple of minutes I suppose, a grayling of some ¾lb as I recall. Quite a few fish were felt on the fly but failed to connect, others connected and were quickly lost, but when I reeled in at the bottom I had six grayling on the bank. It seemed to me just possible that a second spell down the same stretch might prove useful, especially as the breeze at my left back had made casting particularly pleasurable on this stretch. So, beginning again at the top, I once more lengthened line and began working my fly. Notice that the water was quite clear and the light good, so it was not a matter of fishing a spate. When I again reached the bottom of the stretch I had grassed six more fish, many of which came from pockets of water in which I had lost fish on the first traverse. A third passage down produced four more grayling and at that I decided to call it a day. But let me point out that these sixteen fish were not in a shoal in strict terms, but were the normal citizens of that stretch of water. I have fished it many times both before and since, and although it is normally good for the odd fish, the experience of that day has never been repeated. I may add that the last four fish were all returned since I had no desire to 'clean out' the stretch of water and I had only a limited number of friends who liked to eat grayling.

My second memory is very different in that it concerns a wet and stormy day on a very small Perthshire loch. Again it was a loch which I knew well, having shared it with a pair of shoveller ducks and an odd goosander on many previous occasions. Not that its fish merited such close attention, for they were small and not very numerous, but the water was such a joy to fish that I kept returning. The day permit obtainable in Perth (no longer, I regret to add) gave one exclusive fishing of the entire water for the day! My normal catch would be one or two fish, sometimes more.

This day was a disaster weather-wise, with scudding rainstorms pursuing one another across a lowering sky and a high blustery wind bending even the pines and larches. The sort of day when those who know nothing of angling remark that 'it's a grand day for fishing', and those experienced in the sport watch a rugby international on the television. My temporary eccentricity was explained by a long enforced lack of fishing followed by a free day amidst the many other conflicting demands of a family holiday. So off I went with much borrowed rainproof clothing to my little loch amongst the hills.

By the time I reached the waterside I was sodden, with water trickling down the inside of my back, pools of water in my pockets, but, thank Heaven, dry feet. Casting was well-nigh impossible but I attached a team of three small wet flies and allowed the wind to hurl them on to the waters. Almost immediately the truth revealed itself. It was one of those days. The trout, smallish by southern standards, were ready to take anything, and every second cast or so was rewarded with a sturdy half-pounder. I finally reeled in when I was as watery as the fish, my game bag was wetter outside than in, and all semblance of hackle had been worn from my flies. But my bag was heavy with fish and I returned home with a song in my heart to entrench the conviction amongst those at home that the ways of fish and fishermen alike are beyond rationality. Or, to express it in the language of the Celts, they are fickle and fey!

We return southwards for my last narrative, to a rare day on the Test above Romsey in late May, coolish, blustery, but with an early hatch of the real thing, the green drake Mayfly dun, *Ephemera danica*. True to all the stories, the trout had gone mad. I was using an imitation which I knew to be a killer in such circumstances, a large wingless fly tied with the speckled neck feathers of guinea fowl. The fish were lunging at the flies, crossing four feet of pool to take them on the side and, a style of behaviour I have only occasionally encountered elsewhere (and that chiefly with sea trout in lochs), jumping clear of the water and grabbing the fly on the way down! Two brace was my limit and I had to stop in half an hour or less, but it was a sight to see and a memory to cherish.

These then are a few of my memories, snatched from half a lifetime of fishing, contrasting with innumerable fishless days spent in quest of uninterested uncooperative quarry. My memories are far from unusual, I know, and I quote them simply to help stimulate your recall of similar days with eager fish. But it all adds up to the amazing conundrum of the feeding behaviour of fish, and what it is which provokes such carefree rising on one day; such gut-shy reticence on the next.

Now I cannot pretend that either in the guise of scientist or philosophic fisherman I am going to be able to entirely explain the whimsy of the rise; the unpredictability of piscatorial feeding behaviour. But I think that we can at least reduce the enigma even if we cannot remove it entirely. I therefore offer to you, a series of six factors which, along with many others of a lesser impact, partially explain the erratic nature of fish response.

Available food

In some lakes and rivers there is scarcely sufficient food for survival of the fishy occupants. This state of affairs obtains in some desolate peat lochs, some gravelly spate rivers, and many artificially over-stocked gravel pits and lakes. In these situations fish must look for food most of the time in order to survive. Even here, however, there are times when the fish will ignore all baits, natural and artificial. But by contrast, some fisheries are blest with abundant natural food and the resident fish can easily afford to be choosy and to adhere to particular meal-times. It is a contrast between the bushmen of the Kalahari Desert, forced to spend most of the daylight hours in hunting and food-gathering, and the wealthy tycoon holidaying on the French Riviera, who only eats in order to relieve boredom. We can therefore conclude that availability of natural food enforces limitations or permits licence in the fishy tendency not to eat between meals.

Hatches

Some important items of the diet of trout and grayling are themselves subject to fantastic fluctuations in numbers and availability. As with the fish, so with these organisms, we do not necessarily understand why they hatch one day and not the next, nor what induces such incredible synchrony in their appearance. But it is clear that fish can only feed on them when they are available, so the appearance of a hatch of duns always brings a quickening of the pulse for the expectant angler. It is therefore obvious that the feeding behaviour of carnivorous fish often involves a response to the appearance of desirable prey; midge pupae, sedges, mayfly or flying ants.

Otherwise engaged

A frequent reason for a blank afternoon at the riverside or on the hard seat of a Loch Leven boat must be that the fish are occupied totally in pursuit or quest of some food item quite alien to our flies or lures. That is a conclusion which emerges strongly from the analysis of game fish diet in Chapter 6. We could ask whether there is evidence that trout or grayling do feed on snail, *Gammarus*, caddis fly larvae, or Chironomid larvae to the temporary exclusion of all else. After all, these foods must be there for the gathering at any time the individual fish cares to seek them out. But the answer is, I think, strongly in the affirmative. I have myself seen large numbers of trout upended with tails breaking the surface and their noses in the gravel, and the behaviour has continued for over an hour. Analysis of stomach contents also helps confirm this. This is not to deny that while some fish are concentrating on *Daphnia* others may be seeking midge pupae, but simply to state that at certain times most of the fish in one stretch of river or section of a lake may be so occupied in exploiting one food source that our flies, imitating another, will be totally ignored.

Temperature

Numerous climatic factors affect the feeding behaviour of fish, but their importance is somewhat problematical. Wind, sunshine, barometric pressure, thunder, phases of the moon, even perhaps sunspot activity, have all been suggested as trigger factors in turning fish on or off the feed. As far as trout and grayling are concerned, perhaps temperature, and by this we must mean water temperature, is more significant than any other single climatic factor. This is not surprising when we remember that fish are 'cold-blooded', that is, they take their body temperature from the surrounding media, and so when the water is at 4°C. the metabolism of the fish is low, its muscles will not work very efficiently, and it probably will not feed readily. On the other hand, grayling seem to feed more actively at these sorts of temperature than when it rises above 15°C.

Although trout are normally disinclined to feed when the water temperature falls too low, they are even more off-the-feed when it is too high, say above 25°C. The optimum seems to lie between 7 and 15°C., but feeding behaviour in regard to temperature is very variable at different times of the year. In early spring, perhaps due to hunger, trout may feed actively at 3°C., but in late May and June, at least in many lakes and streams, they will refuse food if the temperature drops below 10°C. or rises above 19°C.

What temperature means to the angler is, I think, fairly simple. If you arrive at a lake in summer and find that the water temperature is above 20°C., I suggest you go off for a round of golf, and come back hoping for a drop in the evening. On the other hand, we can all recall times fishing a really active evening rise, when quite suddenly the temperature drops and the rise stops. This again is a time to pack up rod and reel. But conversely, if an Indian summer merges into a warm autumn, the grayling may never feed really actively until November. It will be a perceptive angler who goes out in quest of grayling after the first really cold night, for the drop in water temperature seems to sharpen their appetite.

Having claimed that water temperature is the most significant of the climatic factors affecting the feeding of fish, I should perhaps weaken that assertion a little by saying that many keepers and fishermen, myself amongst them, suspect that changes in barometric pressure are also very important.

Time of day and time of year

The availability of food varies greatly at different times of the year, and fish are profoundly affected in their behaviour by these fluctuations. For example, up until the end of May, even in the south of England, trout will feed sporadically throughout the day, with maximum activity around midday and cessation of feeding at perhaps 6 p.m. Then in June the evening rise begins to appear and feeding comes to be concentrated into midday and evening feeding. By July and August food is often so abundant that the evening rise may be the only intense activity of the day, although frequently early morning feeding may also be encountered. September normally sees a diminution in the importance of the evening rise and more general feeding at noon and afternoon.

Now all of these comments are very much generalisations, and tend to refer most markedly to observable feeding, especially to surface fly. Where trout are hungry they may feed throughout the day, other factors being favourable.

Grayling are no less temperamental than trout in their feeding activity. Their behaviour resembles the trout in the 'back-end' of the year, but feeding intensifies in October when that of the trout is diminishing. October and November will, in reasonable weather, see feeding of grayling at noon and afternoon, with often a vigorous though brief evening rise. The latter will have ceased in December, and over Christmas and January feeding grayling are most in evidence from 11 a.m. until 2.30 p.m. But many exceptions exist, and some anglers do well early in the morning and, especially in mild weather, the bait may be taken very actively until dusk.

Communal behaviour

The feeding frenzy of the shark is known even to the ten-year-old cinema addict, but it is less widely appreciated that many other fish species are stimulated to feed by another's activity. Many fishermen have noticed that rainbow trout, especially when recently introduced to a lake, will move as a shoal and indulge, in the shoal, in communal feeding activity. In these conditions it may pay to cast one's fly or lure exactly in the area from which one has newly extracted a fish (although comments about fishing in goldfish bowls are hard to suppress here).

What is less obvious but almost certainly true, is that well-established fish in a lake, and naturally-bred brown trout in a river, remain to an extent a shoal, though a widely dispersed one. Many are within sight of one another, and it would be no surprise to find that non-visual signals are also exchanged between neighbouring fish in both stillwaters and streams. It follows from this that the feeding impulse may spread amongst trout and grayling like a sudden infection, one fish triggering off another. As I shall stress later in this chapter, the behaviour of fish is much less complex than our own; more a matter of behavioural reflexes to fixed stimuli (like our salivation at the smell of good food) than a carefully thought out procedure. We can therefore conclude that although trout and grayling do, in certain circumstances, have regular meal-times, their response to 'what is on the table' is a behavioural reflex response to a summation of many factors.

A closer look at the feeding reflex

I now propose to take a closer look at the feeding behaviour of trout and grayling, partly because it is interesting in its own right, but particularly because it has many implications for us as fishermen. At the end of this chapter I think that many of my readers may fish differently (and, I trust, more profitably) or at least think differently about the way in which they fish. Since I want to discuss fish behaviour at a fairly basic level, I will approach the subject somewhat tangentially by taking a broad look at animal behaviour in general.

The study of animal behaviour has been one of the great growth points in biology and psychology over the past two or three decades, and we as fishermen would do well to reap the benefit of this advance. Behavioural responses of animals have come to be understood as falling into distinct categories. On the one hand animals may have an inborn reaction to a stimulus, with little or no overlay of modification by experience or intellectual thought. In short, this is *instinctive* behaviour. At the other end of the scale is a reaction which may result from learning by the individual or may have a considerable intellectual aspect. This, in short, is *acquired* behaviour. I must hasten to point out that this subdivision of behaviour is very oversimplified and I am tending to lump together aspects of behaviour which do not necessarily go hand in hand. Thus I have suggested that *acquired* behaviour is not only non-reliant on instinct but is also likely to involve intellectual consideration. This does not always follow. A first division footballer may owe much of his skill to learning, but, once learned, the actual responses can become rapid and *reflex* rather than always requiring the time-consuming element of thought. So learned behaviour may begin as a slow thoughtful response, but with practice it may develop into something as fast and 'automatic' as much instinctive behaviour.

As animals go, and here we can most conveniently confine ourselves to vertebrates (that is, everything between a fish and a mammal on the evolutionary scale), the human is without doubt the greatest exponent of acquired learned behaviour and the least reliant on instinct. But even the human species display instinctive behaviour. The baby's smile, the suckling response, salivation on scenting food, raising of the eyebrows as a greeting – all of these are commonly looked on as simple examples of human instinctive behaviour, unlearned and universal. More complex examples of instinctive behaviour in other animals include the ability of a swallow or cuckoo, born in rural Yorkshire, to find its way to South Africa and back without map, compass, or even the help of the older birds (young birds in their first year leave *after* the parents and make the flight totally unaided by experience). Science has now shown that most migratory birds are born with an innate knowledge of celestial navigation, so that they can find direction by studying the night sky. The signals which are used by migratory salmon in finding their native river remain largely obscure although smell seems to play a part once they are in the approximate vicinity of their native estuary.

A further interesting aspect to animal behaviour is that, especially with instinctive response, there are often simple signals which act as 'releasers' of that particular behaviour pattern. So we can call the smell of food a releaser for the salivation response, and we could proceed to test different

Fig. 7.1 Photograph of an adult meadow pipit feeding a young cuckoo which it has fostered at the expense of its own youngster. The meadow pipit is actually standing on the young cuckoo's back in order to present food to the adopted fledgling. This behaviour dramatically illustrates the fact that many animals may show normal behavioural responses, such as feeding young, in response to stimuli which seem a grotesque abstraction of the normal 'releasing' situation. By the same token fish may take as food lures which have little direct resemblance to normal food organisms, but may nevertheless release the feeding response very powerfully.

smells to find which were the most effective. Now here we encounter a weird and often amusing aspect of behaviour, namely that the factor which elicits a particular response, i.e. the releaser, may be at its most effective when it becomes quite abnormal and even appears to be an absurd caricature of normality. For example, robins set up territories in winter and so individual robins are often very aggressive to one another at this time. A dead stuffed robin will be attacked vigorously by other male robins, so suggesting that at this time of the year the appearance of a male robin 'releases' the aggressive behaviour. But it turns out that a whole stuffed robin is not necessary, only the red breast, so that aggression in male robins will be displayed towards a quite grotesque model with a red breast, but not at all to complete stuffed copies without red breasts.

Two other examples from the bird world are worth quoting since they help to establish in our minds the simplistic nature of many instinctive behaviour patterns. The first is illustrated in *Fig. 7.1* and involves the development of the young cuckoo in the nest of a small bird such as a meadow pipit. Parent meadow pipits feed their young as part of an instinctive response, so that if a young cuckoo hatches in the nest, it will not only be fed too, but will be fed preferentially because, being bigger, it presents a number of releasing signals in exaggerated form. The upshot of this situation is that the young cuckoo, having replaced the original brood and outgrown the rest, may be perched on a tree stump, being patiently or even frantically fed by two meadow pipits who are so much smaller than the cuckoo that they must perch on its shoulder to get food into its mouth! This is an absurd demonstration of reflex behaviour being effectively released by a highly exaggerated stimulus.

My second example is a somewhat similar situation, this time involving the egg-brooding behaviour of a common shore bird, the oystercatcher. It appears that the shape and colour of the egg act as releasing stimuli for brooding behaviour, so that if a giant egg of the correct shape and colour is provided, the bird will brood that in preference to its own egg (see *Fig. 7.2*) even if it means straddling the egg so that both feet are off the ground! The giant egg exaggerates the shape and colour stimuli and is thus a better releaser of brooding behaviour.

Now where does all this detour into bird behaviour get us? I think it establishes that much behaviour in the vertebrates is instinctive and therefore that these animals may be turned on

Fig. 7.2 Diagram of an oyster catcher attempting to incubate a grossly oversized artificial egg in preference to its own. The oversized egg presents a stronger stimulus than the natural.

to a particular behaviour pattern by stimuli which seem to us to bear little resemblance to the original basic releaser. This is not to deny that learning may not modify much of this behaviour. The meadow pipit no doubt has to learn how to balance on a young cuckoo's shoulder, but the basic feeding response is in answer to a signal beyond rationality – the bird is driven by its inheritance to act in this way and has no real choice in the matter. But we are not here supposed to be discussing bird behaviour but fish behaviour; our aim is to catch trout, not oystercatchers. Where does our friend the fish come out in all this?

There is no question but that fish behaviour is very largely instinctive, even if there is an overlay of learned behaviour superimposed on it. This implies that when we are thinking about the behavioural responses of fish we would be best to have in our minds the idea of a reflex action triggered off by a releasing stimulus, rather than the carefully considered cerebral response that is the common human situation with which we are all acquainted. The view that fish behaviour is largely instinctive is now supported by a large body of evidence, only a little of which I will trouble you with here. But some is certainly very relevant to our topic.

One of the fathers of modern animal behaviour is Professor Niko Tinbergen and back in the 1940's he carried out some intriguing experiments with sticklebacks. Male sticklebacks are known to be highly territorial and aggressive to one another in the breeding season. Tinbergen became interested in precisely what, in one male stickleback, acted as the aggression-releasing stimulus for the second fish. As shown in *Fig. 7.3* he made a series of model sticklebacks, some closely resembling the live fish in size and shape, others of quite different shapes. He discovered that authentic looking stickleback models without red breasts were poor releasers, but that models which bore no real resemblance to a stickleback would act as powerful releasers provided their bellies were coloured red. In other words, the red belly is the key stimulus, just as the shape and colour of the egg is to the brooding oystercatcher.

The implications of this discovery for our fishing techniques are of the greatest importance. It tells us that a lure or fly need not be a faithful copy of the genuine article to elicit a good feeding response, and indeed that lures quite unlike any known prey organism may evoke feeding by the fish more effectively than the real thing. To return to the oystercatcher straddling the impossibly large egg, lures of absurd construction may prove effective, provided – by accident or design – they include in their appearance some releasing stimulus for feeding behaviour.

Of course, there is no denying that trout and grayling can be very fastidious in their selection of food organisms and in rejection of our authentic looking artificials. But the point I am making is that, to the fish, total resemblance may not be important, but presence of certain essential stimulatory signals may. I should hasten to add that we only know in shadowy

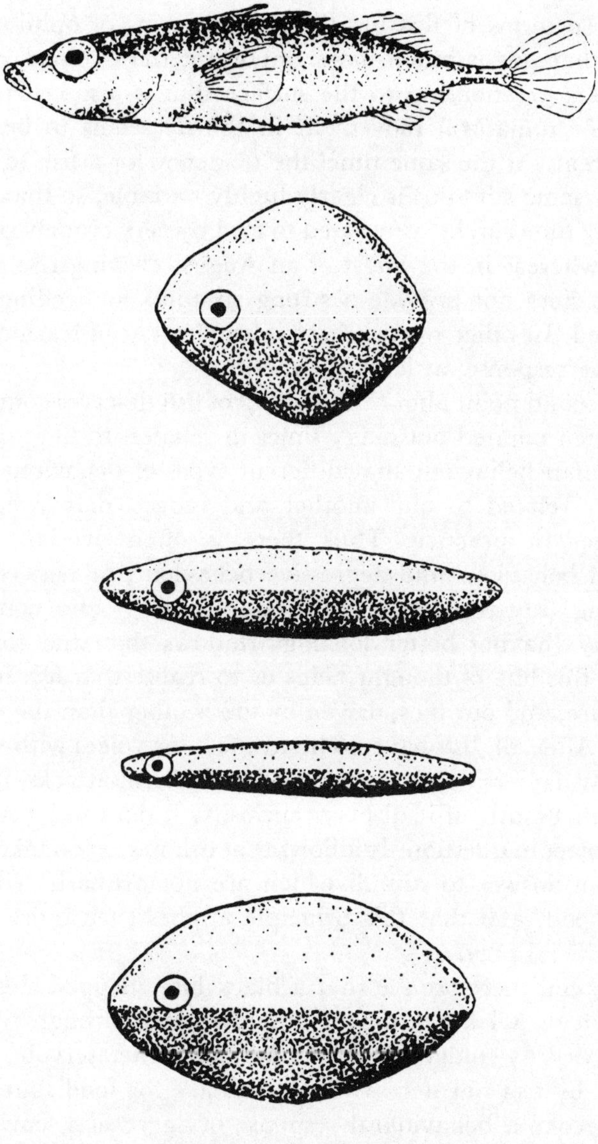

Fig. 7.3 Models of sticklebacks used to evoke aggressive response by male sticklebacks. Provided a red breast is present, shape seems to be irrelevant to the response.

terms what turns trout and grayling on and induces them to feed. In terms of floating flies, a consensus of opinion would hold that size is much more important than colour, and that the flies' relationship to the surface film is also crucial. Thus drag or unnatural movement in the fly seems to be a great deterrent. At the same time, the tendency for a fish to respond to the same stimulus is clearly highly variable, so that trout at mayfly time can be stimulated to feed by very crudely presented flies, whereas in the midst of an August evening rise anything which does not provide a strong stimulus for feeding will be ignored. In other words, there is an element of learning in the feeding response, at least at times.

A second point about the feeding of fish deserves comment. It has been pointed out many times in relation to the psychology of human behaviour that different types of behaviour may be closely related to one another and indeed may overlap one another in practice. Thus there is often overlap between sexual behaviour and aggressive behaviour, or between home making (say repainting the front windows) and competitive display (having better looking windows than the Jones's). I think this line of thought helps us to realise that fish may take our lure, and our flies, driven by urges other than the quest for food. After all, fish have no hands, feet, or voices with which to display aggression, or even curiosity. If a fish attacks, it does so with its mouth; if it displays curiosity, it does so by mouthing the object in question. It follows that fish may even take natural prey in answer to stimuli which are not primarily concerned with food, and that this principle applies even more strongly to artificial prey.

We can therefore see that a black lure stripped close to the bottom of a lake; a devon minnow spun through a pool; a large dry fly nudged over the surface of a reservoir; may be taken by fish not necessarily in mistake for food, but because they evoke a behavioural response of aggression, curiosity, or of course feeding – or all three! As we have discussed above, different behavioural patterns may overlap. The ideal fish attractant would be one which elicited responses for feeding, attack, and inquisitiveness simultaneously. Rather like the ideal car which is roomy enough for the children, comfortable enough for one's wife, fast and sporty as an appeal to male competitiveness, and cheap enough to be purchasable. Much of that type of behaviour, that is car purchase, involves intellectual choice (though probably less than we think), but you must adopt the philosophy of the car salesman when trying to beguile fish into your bag, knowing also that their behavioural reactions will be even more programmed and less considered than that of the human car-purchaser.

There is more to fish behaviour than pure instinct, however, for fish can learn both what to eat and what to avoid. But once more we should not think of their learning as being much akin to our slow and thoughtful acquisition of experience. Rather it should be seen, in the jargon of the psychologist, as the acquisition of 'conditioned reflexes'. By this it is meant that if an animal is repeatedly rewarded or punished after a certain pattern of behaviour, the pattern can be modified, or in other words the animal learns to do one thing or not to do another. It is conditioned reflex behaviour that is involved in trout learning to use automatic feeders, to recognise pellets as food, or even to become tame. By the same token it is presumably conditioned reflexes which make fish 'gut shy', or which render them difficult to deceive with artificial flies if they have been hooked on them three or four times. But the acquisition of these conditioned responses take time and repetition, and fish, hooked once by an artificial fly, should hardly be expected to become instantly wary of other artificials.

Let us now sum up this section from the standpoint of the angler. The following points represent the main conclusions.

—Fish are likely to take flies and lures both as feeding behaviour and also as part of aggressive or 'curiosity-satisfying' behaviour.

—'Artificials' bearing no obvious resemblance to natural prey will be taken, often in preference to the latter.

—The design of artificial flies, baits and lures should involve attempts to discover and copy releasing stimuli in prey organisms. (Grayling are said to favour dry flies with a touch of red colour.)

—Fish are capable of learning, but only after repeated stimulation by 'reward' or 'punishment', and their learned responses are not 'thought out'.

—Trout, both brown and sea trout, when caught on devon minnows or spoons, are probably not exhibiting a feeding response but, as with salmon taking flies or spoons, displaying either aggressive or inquisitive behaviour or some mixture of the two.

So this chapter has not provided a universal panacea for the problems of anglers or the prevention of blank days, but I think I can fairly say that it points in the right direction.

8
The Fish's Environment

How can I forget my schoolboy fishing trips in the environs of Edinburgh? Clutching my home-made greenheart rod in one hand and a small haversack slung over my shoulder, I trudged the heathery moors, sound of snipe and curlew overhead, to the infant stream which later became the Water of Leith. Its sparkling shallows and mysterious pools were a constant source of adventure and delight, and although I commonly plodded back over the moor with no fish, and wet feet, while my boots slopped with the misfortunes of that day, my mind was already preoccupied with the business of planning another such trip on the next.

As time passed and circumstances changed I came to savour the delights of other waters. The splendid wet and dry fly fishing on the broad waters of the Aberdeenshire Don; worming in both clear and spate waters of many Highland burns. My first trips abroad brought an introduction to the cold rivers of Norwegian Lapland, then teeming with Arctic char, and even some fishing trips on the noble rivers and lakes of the United States. My earliest contact with the gracious grayling was in the border Tweed, at first caught by mistake (and some disappointment) when trouting, but latterly pursued with care and respect and most frequently a small dry fly. The Tweed then – between twenty and thirty years ago – was a splendid river, shallow enough to wade in the gravelly stretches, strong and deep in the pools. The summer days seemed hot and still, but always with the promise of an evening rise to follow. Even on the hottest days, hard work and much scrambling up banks, over the numerous boulders of Tweed's valley, would be rewarded by the always breathtaking discovery of a feeding trout in the deep shade of an overhanging tree. I spent many afternoons trying to cover such fish with my somewhat crudely-tied flies. My biggest Tweed trout of those days was $1\frac{1}{4}$lb (though there were many bigger) and grayling of around $\frac{3}{4}$lb, but then I had much to learn.

Latterly I have savoured the thick weedbeds and crystal clear waters of Hampshire chalk streams, Meon, Avon, Itchen and Test, together with many days on reservoirs and lakes, both stocked and unstocked. My chalk stream fishing has all been on the cheap, as necessitated by my purse, but none the less I have come to love these peaceful river valleys with their weedbeds and water meadows (see *Plate 6*), and never least in autumn and winter, when, with maggots and flies, I go after the grayling again.

As I sit at my table and write, even now fishing memories come flooding into my mind at the least invitation, and always they are rich in detail of the environment of fishing; of quiet weed-fringed corners of reservoirs tenanted by secretive giant trout which sip *caenis* in the fading light of July evenings; of remote Highland lochs reached only by weary battles with tall heather and ridges, but mysterious in their peaty stillness, with groups of water lilies, and yellow asphodels and fragrant bog myrtle underfoot. I am certain that I share many memories with you of large fish lost in tangled under-river roots of alder trees; of the creak of oars on endless reservoirs, where it blows either force eight or not at all; of vast fly hatches when fishing proves fruitless and we become mere admirers of the miracle of hatching duns and hungry fish. For many of us fishing is oft a spectator sport, as we munch our sandwiches or await the afternoon rise of fish; at such times who of us does not feel a part of the world of the dabchicks and water voles, share a sense of kinship when we catch a rare flash of the master fisherman, the kingfisher, or surprise the careful heron at his game.

It is obviously easy enough to wax lyrical about the environment of the fish, for that provides much of the joy of fishing. Who would go a-fishing if it implied casting flies over concrete-sided pools, or searching out the depths of storage tanks with float tackle? Trout and grayling live in an aquatic environment, thereby giving us excuse for enjoying some of the finest scenery which our countryside affords. As fishermen, we become involved in the countryside in a manner shared by few other sports. We jump ditches, wade cautiously through shallows, even at times crawl (unseen we hope) on all fours in attempts to sight our fish and work out a strategy for its capture. The next time you emerge soaked in chilling water and trailing a mass of soggy weeds, do not curse your carelessness at falling in, but reflect on your deep intimacy with the world of your quarry! We do not just admire Nature; we grasp and grapple with her.

Fishing affords another peculiar advantage to the countryman. If you wander through villages or by watersides alone, you will be regarded as an object of suspicion by adults and children alike. This is the unfortunate fate of the lone walker or naturalist. But with a fishing rod all is transformed. Fishermen are universally regarded as perhaps odd but benevolent and harmless. If you stand and stare as a stream flows by, you may be thought strange to the point of lunacy, and the local constabulary may be called, but with a fishing rod all is forgiven. What you are doing may be not understood but it is universally accepted as being harmless. So, fellow fishermen, there is much to be said for our particular relationship with the fish's environment.

Let us now be somewhat more serious in considering the fish's environment and discuss together some of the interesting aspects of rivers and lakes which hold grayling or trout.

Grayling waters

As I mentioned in Chapter 1, the grayling is a European fish but probably not a native British one. Its supposed introduction to Britain has led to a very uneven distribution so that it occurs only in a few of the waters truly suited to it (see *Table 1.1*). Grayling thrive in fast streaming water, well supplied with oxygen, and supporting a prolific weed growth. They seem to do best in alkali waters such as the limestone and chalk streams, although there are many grayling in neutral waters such as Tweed and Tay. Their demand for a fast current and good oxygenation means that the best parts of a river for grayling may often be upstream of the optimal trout stretches, although obviously a lot of overlap occurs. In rivers like Tay and Tweed the grayling are not found in the feeder streams since these are often somewhat acid, shallow and short of weed. In a phrase, they tend to be spate rivers. So the grayling zones of these rivers are the broad slower middle reaches. Conversely, in the chalk stream grayling are plentiful in small feeder streams and become scarce in the last few miles of slower deeper river channels. My ideal grayling water would be not more than twenty feet across, with a depth range of three to five feet and plenty of groins and weirs, a gravel bed and luxuriant weedbeds.

Grayling are highly mobile fish, and less territorial than their cousin the trout. This tendency towards a nomadic life is especially evident in winter, when they often disappear from pools which they frequent in summer and early autumn and congregate in shoals in deeper water. I find this very perplexing as a fisherman for the fish do not now betray their presence by surface feeding, and must be sought patiently with float tackle and maggot or worm baits. Many blank days appear in my fishing diary in quest of winter grayling, but when you do find them you may collect quite a few fish.

Another point worth making is that the large grayling appear to be much more solitary and, although they may be taken on the dry fly, they are most likely to be caught by dropping a suitable bait, well weighted, some five or six feet into quiet eddies and slacks at the junction of faster currents.

Sensitivity to even low levels of pollution seems to be a special characteristic of grayling and they may therefore represent a much better natural pollution monitor than the trout. Recent reduction in grayling numbers in the Hampshire Avon and Test has been noted by many fishermen, but whether pollution is the factor here one cannot easily determine. I strongly suspect that a more likely reason is high summer temperatures. Grayling basically are fish of temperate and alpine waters and do not thrive above 16°C. Certainly the poor growth of grayling in July and August is an intriguing observation which may be related to its intolerance of high temperatures.

Trout waters – rivers

As species go, trout are more catholic in their tastes as to acceptable environment than are grayling. The rainbow trout especially seem to be able to adapt to the rivers and lakes into which it is introduced, tolerating some pollution and rather poor levels of oxygenation. Let us first discuss the ideal environment of the brown trout and sea trout, before we discuss the rainbow. As already indicated, trout demand less turbulent waters than grayling, but appreciate rough bottoms, abundant cover, and reasonable flow of water.

Although favouring less turbulent waters than the grayling, trout thrive best in the upper reaches of rivers, amongst hills and mountains. They require a stony or sandy bottom, good oxygenation, and cool temperatures, and so as our rivers descend to the plains and meander slowly between meadows, the trout is largely replaced by roach, rudd and dace. These fish are more tolerant of the muddy bottom and slower flow which characterises such waters. It is possible to think of an average river as being in two sections. One, the upper part, is *eroding* in its action, since silt and stones are being actively carried downstream, at least slowly and occasionally. The other, the *depositing* zone, is the stretch of river where the eroded material can settle out and the bottom will tend to be muddy (this terminology was first used, I think, by the fish biologist H. B. Hynes). Trout characteristically occupy the *eroding* section of a river system.

It must be added that in many mountainous areas the water run off is extremely rapid, especially where the river beds are rocky and steep. Such rivers scour the bed very severely when in flood, and are then prone to dry up almost to extinction in dry weather. Fish cannot thrive in such waters (although sea trout and salmon often use them for spawning and ascend at times of flood). So you should be cautious not to waste your time paying for a trout permit on a river whose nature makes the life of the brown trout almost impossible.

Brown trout are extremely territorial in rivers, and each fish will have a lair to which it retreats when not feeding, and only one or two regular feeding stations. Other trout are only tolerated at certain times and under certain conditions within the territory.

Experienced fishermen know as if by instinct where trout can be expected to feed in a stream. Remember that early in the season they may select slack water and the middle or tail of a run, but as they gain strength and the season advances, the larger fish may take up turbulent water in the neck of a run. If the river you fish has abundant weedbeds, seek your feeding fish just below the weedbeds, where currents both on and below the surface will concentrate nymphs and hatching flies into a narrow funnel. In fishing very small streams one has to seek fish in the necks of large pools, since often these are the only positions affording both food and cover. Any trout stream of less than twenty feet across will have 90 per cent of its brown trout population feeding beside or even under the banks, always assuming there is deepish water there, and often only at dusk will they take up central or exposed feeding positions. On larger rivers, on the other hand, cover may be available mid-river, under weed or boulder, and the banks will prove much less productive.

Sea trout inhabit rivers at spawning times which are quite incapable of supporting a viable population of the adults the year round. Thus the famous sea trout rivers are often very fast spate rivers, ascended by the trout in times of flood in order to find the gravelly upper reaches ideal for spawning. So you must seek your sea trout in large slacks and eddies, especially at the tails of pools and under trees, and expect the fish to be slightly shoaling in habit while they await further rain to encourage the run upstream. Of course, sea trout also run up good brown trout rivers and may then be found rising to fly just like the non-migratory browns.

I well remember fishing dry fly on the Aberdeenshire Don one August evening. The river above Inverurie is wide and often deep, and holds many salmon, besides being an excellent trout water. A long deep glide along my own bank often attracted feeding trout in the evening and I crept up to survey it, with only some Fresians for company. More than one fish seemed to be feeding (it is easy to be fooled, though, since sometimes one fish is feeding on a ranging circuit; at other times, especially when food is very abundant, two or three fish may feed very close together), and I chose the nearer rise as being the bigger fish. A ¾lb brown quickly came to the net. The presence of two fish was now obvious, since tiny sipping rises continued some yards further up the glide. To be honest, I cannot remember casting to the fish in detail – how memory is obliterated by startling events – for minutes later I had tightened not into another little brown, but into something of real substance. I recalled my tiny hook with anxiety, and why had I failed to take that wind knot out of the leader? As the fish tore away I guessed that I was at last connected to one of the legendary giant brown trout of the Don – even the word salmon flashed through my mind – but a moment later the flash of leaping silver eliminated the first possibility. Indeed, I was a trifle disappointed at its size, for its weight felt like something over 6lbs, yet when I finally eased it over the net it proved to be a fine sea trout of 3½lbs. They were then uncommon in the Don and I was delighted with my catch, which I proudly displayed to my landlord and friends back at the Banks Of Urie Hotel.

So much for the sea trout, sometimes a happy surprise while after other game, sometimes hard to rouse in famous sea trout rivers, but always fast and exciting fish.

Trout waters – stillwaters

Most clean and many dirty rivers in Europe contain brown

trout, although they may be small and hungry in the tiny feeder streams, especially in the mountains of Wales and Scotland, and larger and darker in the slow water close to the estuary. But trout are as much a feature of stillwaters as they are of rivers. Indeed more trout fishing by far is now pursued in the latter. What then are the characteristics of good trout lakes, lochs or reservoirs?

The question is complicated greatly by stocking, since there is nothing to prevent a very poor trout water being stocked with 5lb brown and rainbow trout and, provided they are caught soon after entry, they will give the water a high reputation even if the poor fish were miserable in it and never found a blessed thing to eat! All I can do is to indicate what a good trout water should be like to ensure not only survival but growth and development in the trout. The fish require certain essentials – cool, well-oxygenated water with minimum pollution and abundant food. The last factor was discussed at length in Chapter 6, so we pause here only to add that recently flooded land often affords excellent food for a few years, as it did in the great early years of Blagdon reservoir, but this high level is not necessarily sustained. Only a fairly shallow water will allow enough light to the bottom to encourage the prolific weed growth necessary for really abundant trout food, although small lakes surrounded by trees and shrubs may have a rich wind-blown menu to complement what thrives on or near to the bottom.

Since trout are not particularly demanding about the pH of the water, that is its acidity or alkalinity, oxygenation often emerges as the really crucial deciding element in the survival and well-being of the fish populations. Since many factors affect the oyxgen levels, I have listed only the main items involved. Poorly oxygenated lakes will harbour roach, bream, tench and carp, and a fisherman of any experience will quickly know whether the water he is surveying is likely to sustain a good population of trout.

Depth Deep water is likely to be less well oxygenated than shallow. This is not invariably true, but is commonly the case.

Water Disturbance Entry of stream water in a lake will bring oxygenated water, so isolated lakes and lochs with very slow feeder streams may pose problems.

Wind and Rain Surface disturbance by wind and air capture by rain will help to oxygenate lakes, so quiet, still weather may be the difficult time. I wonder if this explains the sudden activity of lake trout during squally showers or in conditions of breaking waves?

Water Plants Here there is a happy medium. Too much weed may pose oxygenation problems especially at night. I am told that in a lake about 60 per cent weed and 40 per cent open space is about right. Plants both use oxygen (during respiration) and produce it (during photosynthesis, the process of starch formation). But the latter can only occur in sunlight so at night plants are a respiratory loss to a lake (consequently problems of low oxygen are worst at night or early morning), but on a bright day may be a slight respiratory gain. These comments also hold true for the small floating algae which may render water like pea soup in hot summers.

Mud A build-up of mud, with lots of decaying leaves, is bad because the bacterial decomposition uses up oxygen.

Pollution Certain types of pollution may rapidly reduce the oxygen level of a lake, especially inflow of nitrogenous fertiliser from agricultural land leading to a sudden bloom of algae and bacteria and a fairly sudden crash in oxygen level following. As I will discuss further in Chapter 9, there is great cause for anxiety over the pollution of many lakes and rivers with agricultural nitrogenous fertiliser washed from fields by rain. These nitrates lead to prolific algal growth in lakes and ultimately result in a reduced oxygen availability. Such waters are then said to be *eutrophic*, and there is plenty of published evidence that even large bodies of water such as Blagdon and Chew are fast heading in that direction.

Ice A thick unbroken cover of ice over a lake for an extended period may lead to a serious fall in its oxygen level and consequent fish death. This is particularly so when the ice is covered by a thick layer of snow which prevents photosynthesis by the plants.

Temperature I have left the most important factor to the end. If a lake remains cool, life is fairly easy for its fishy tenants, but when it warms up it becomes hell. This is because two separate factors combine to render hot water unbearable. Firstly, the oxygen-carrying capacity of water is inversely proportional to temperature. Cold water has lots of oxygen, hot water very little. Have you ever wondered why the sea fisheries of the Arctic are so productive? Secondly, a fish's blood cells can acquire the oxygen more easily at a lower temperature, that is at round 2 to 10°C., than they can at temperatures above that: the precise reason for that was discussed in Chapter 3. But mass deaths of trout in lakes do sometimes occur in prolonged hot still weather, simply because the fish can no longer get enough oxygen to survive.

In summary, we can expect to find healthy lively trout in lakes that are not over-deep, have plenty of water disturbance, are not choked with an overdose of water plants or mud, and remain relatively cool. You can see now why the depth question is also complex, since in a very hot spell a uniformly shallow lake may lose its entire fish population, while a deeper one will get by because the deeper water remains cooler and therefore *better* oxygenated than the shallow.

Conclusion

I hope I have succeeded in persuading my reader that trout and grayling have very distinct preferences and needs, and that understanding these can both enhance your fishing enjoyment and save you wasting your time. Please do not waste your energy and money flogging rivers and lakes for trout, when some intelligent observations could have assured you that the water in question is quite unsuitable for them. If it is a rainbow-stocked stillwater, all right. Rainbows will survive in a sterile swimming pool for a week maybe! But if the water is not substantially stocked, use your eyes and your brains. Very many waters are advertised by hotels and town councils as affording good trout fishing, at a fee, and yet no self-respecting trout would be seen dead in them. So be careful. If you cannot spot live feeding trout, look for other things – a sterile stony bottom is characteristic of a spate river; mud and the presence of roach are indicative of sluggish non-trout waters. Even the landscape geography will help to give you clues, although excellent trout waters are to be found in some surprising places. The worst examples of alleged trout fishing where few or no trout exist are probably in Wales and Scotland, where spate rivers full of salmon parr and silted or peaty lochs devoid of trout are often offered as established trout fisheries to deceive the over-optimistic or unwary fishermen.

9
A Discussion of Fishing Methods

Let me tell you a parable.

One day five men went forth to fish in a certain water, Blagdon by name. That water was known throughout all the land for its stock of very many large fish, and indeed these five men were known to be mighty men with the rod and exceedingly skilful with the angle. When they came to the place where the fish were they unpacked their bags, put up their rods and attached cunningly-crafted flies to their lines. These flies they now cast upon the waters. For a great time they angled in vain and no fish came, but finally one man hooked and caught a fine trout. He was immediately assailed by three of the other men, beseeching him that he reveal to them the name of the fly that had achieved this wondrous success. This he willingly did, telling them that it was called, at least in his own country, a Jersey Herd. These other three men then did immediately search very thoroughly throughout their own fly boxes until they came on one of those same flies, which, with trembling hands, they did tie on to their lines. These Jersey Herd flies then did these three men all cast forth upon the waters with great hope, remembering well that fine fish which their friend had caught. Moreover, most carefully did they fish these flies at precisely the depth and speed used by the first angler when his fly had been so successful, and also, remembering his success, they cast their flies very near to his fly, hoping that they too would be blessed. Meanwhile the fifth angler, who had stayed apart from his fellows, had also heard the troubling of the waters and the capture of the fish and had witnessed the gathering of the anglers which followed. But he, preferring his own judgment, went his way, continuing to fish with a certain nymph fly which he had tied with great cunning, knowing that the fish in those parts fed very readily on such creatures.

Now it came to pass that these five men gathered together in the evening and, conversing together, they haply did exchange accounts of their success. But while the first four anglers, who had fished patiently all day with their Jersey Herds, had but one fish between them, behold the fifth man had many fish, some caught on his cunningly tied nymph, others on divers patterns of fly. It was also revealed that whereas the first four men had chosen to fish only in one part, and that the place from which the first fish had been taken, the fifth man had diligently searched for fish in many places and lo! his search had been richly rewarded.

Therefore I say unto you, blessed is the man who, seeing another catch one or two fish, doth not immediately fish in the same waters with the same fly, but rather, thinking his own thoughts inwardly, doth continue to try with wisdom and observation. For he will be richly rewarded with fish and verily will be a happier man when the end cometh.

I hope the moral from my short story will be obvious, but I would like to expand a little on the statistics of fish catches.

FISHING STRATEGY AND STATISTICS

We have all at some time or another fished on a lake with many boats, only to find that one boat catches four fish, another two, and another one, while the remaining boats, including our own, draws a blank. On such occasions it is noticeable that the angler in the most successful boat is eloquent in praise of his flies and methods of fishing, and is heard with a mixture of interest and envy by the other fishermen. Now the question I want to ask is this. Is it anything but chance? What exactly are

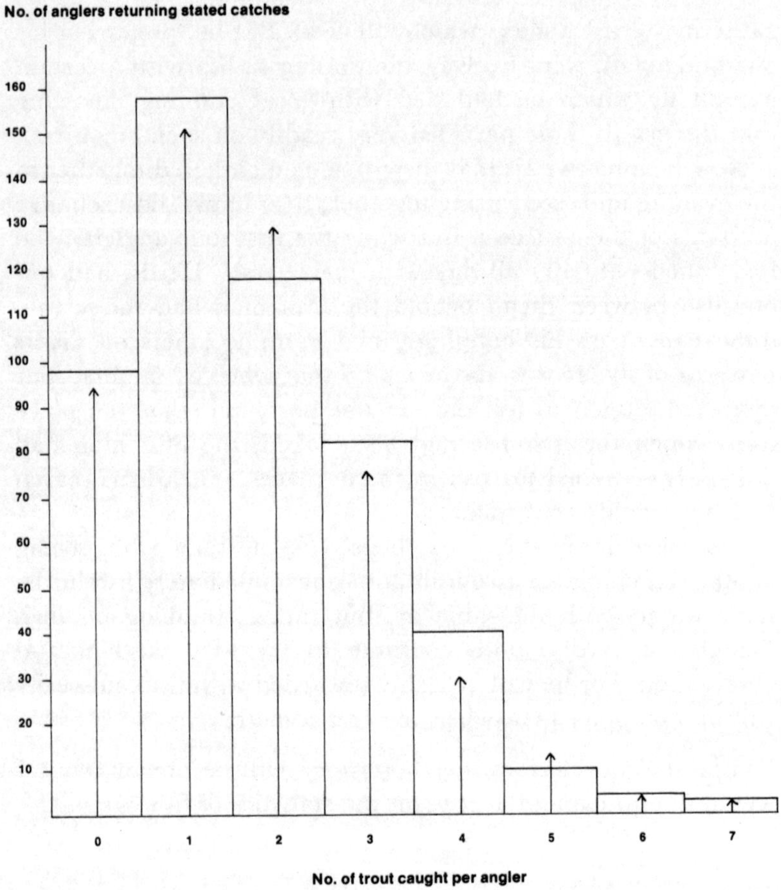

Fig. 9.1 An analysis of the baskets of 512 anglers at a large stillwater fishery. The blocks show the actual numbers of anglers with a particular catch and the arrows the frequencies predicted by a Poisson distribution.

the chances of one man catching four fish and many others none? We could, with patience and determination, work out the answer to this interesting question ourselves by the use of a bag of marbles, but it will be quicker and easier to use the information contained in *Fig. 9.1*. The curve in this figure is

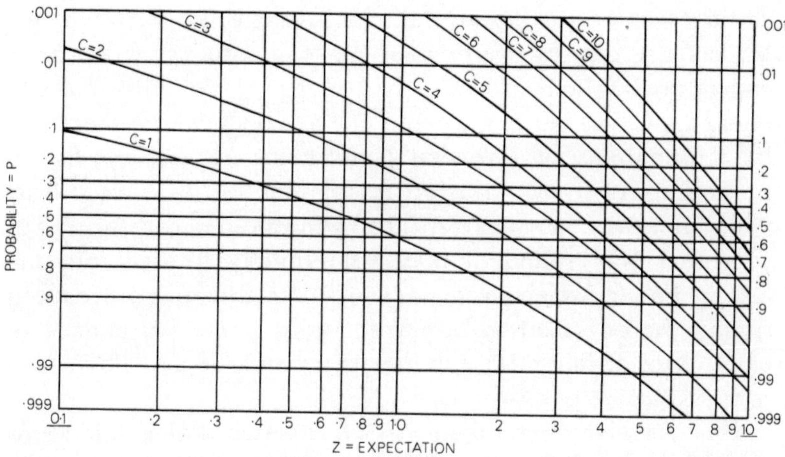

Fig. 9.2 Poisson probability curves. The probability P relates to the number of times (c) that an event will occur out of a total expected number of occurrences (Z). Probabilities are always in terms of something occurring C times or more (i.e. at least C times). If the average catch at a particular fishery is 2 fish per day, then, on chance alone, with Z = 2, the probability of catching at least 2, 60%; of catching at least 3, 30%; of catching at least 4, 15%; of catching at least 5, about 7%. The chances of catching 8 or more are about 1 in 1000. But of course skill or special circumstances (such as restocking the previous day) might modify these expectations considerably.

called a Poisson distribution curve – and the French translation is entirely coincidental! It can be used to determine the frequency distributions of many different variables, whether they be the number of goals scored at football matches or the number of fish caught by fishermen. For our purposes, however, it is the information which we can derive from such a curve that is of the greatest interest. *Fig. 9.2* is somewhat more complex, but much more useful and informative. From it we can deduce the probabilities of catching certain numbers of fish, assuming that all fishermen fish with equal skill and variation in the catch is determined purely by chance. Thus if the average catch at a certain lake is, say, one fish between two anglers per day (a pretty poor place, I admit), what can I expect my bag to be if I have an average fishing ability? Z will equal 0.5 ($\frac{1}{2}$ fish per angler) and one can deduce that there will be a probability of 4:10 that I will catch at least one fish, a probability of 9:100 (nearly 1 in 10) that I will catch at least two, but only 2:100 (1 in 50) that I will catch at least three. Put the other way round, a man who smugly strolled into the fishing hut to weigh in a catch of three fish may have been simply the one man in fifty who was destined by chance to catch three or more fish. On the other hand, he may have been more skilful!

If we now consider a water which is better stocked and sends the average angler away with a bag of two good fish, what will the spread of catches be? The answer is that there is nearly a 9 out of 10 chance of catching at least one fish; a 6 out of 10 chance of catching at least two fish; 3 out of 10 of catching at least three fish; better than 1 in 10 of catching at least four fish, and about 7 in 100 of catching at least five fish. Rather less than 1 in 100 will catch six or more fish.

We can conclude from all these figures that if a man strolls home at the first fishery with four or more fish he is beginning to look like a more successful fisher than average, since there is only 1 chance in 500 that he could do it by luck alone. Similarly, in the second fishery the man who returns with a basket of eight fish has only a 1 in 1000 chance of accomplishing it through random causes and is most likely to be more skilful than average. But the main message is, do not be too hasty in assuming that more fish necessarily means more skill. Only *consistently* more fish puts special angling skill seriously beyond the explanation of luck.

The next time you go a-fishing, however, do not spend too much time pondering my figures as you work your flies. If you do, as you miss the only offer of the day you will be left with an even more difficult equation to solve. Did you lose the fish through bad luck or poor fishing skill? I leave you to solve that one if you can; I gave it up years ago! But before we leave our facts and figures I would like to make one more point. If you are appraising a new fishery and examining the game book (and I hope you do that, for all good fisheries should keep a meticulous record of catches and the sensible angler can learn much from its perusal) remember that the figures we have been conjuring with are based on an assumption of all anglers having the same average ability. If a fishery shows two fish per angler per day, but one or two anglers consistently catch most of these fish, then the caught fish are not distributed randomly between the anglers. You might easily join and find that, if you do your sums carefully, you have less than 1 chance in 50 of catching even one fish. You have been warned!

Another small comment about fishing mathematics is the importance of maximising the chances of fish and hook making contact in space. When fishing some waters, a little arithmetic could convince us that the fish density per cubic yard of water is so low that there is very little chance of fish and fly even being in the same locality together. This implies that no matter how attractive the lure, how exact an imitation the fly, we may catch no fish simply because the latter never catches sight of the former. I recall some years ago holidaying on the Isle of Jura and spending a considerable amount of time sea fishing in a particular shallow bay, with long lines worked from a dinghy. Never a bite did we have in three days, no matter how fresh and tempting our bait. Finally we were joined by other friends who had brought with them some subaqua equipment and, since at that time I belonged to a subaqua club, I joined these people in an exploration of our bay. To my considerable amazement I discovered the reason for our lack of fishing success. There were just no fish there!

The other side of this coin is to emphasise that where you see evidence of the presence of fish in stream or reservoir, it is always advisable to put the fly or bait in that vicinity, even if the fish are not apparently taking the represented organism at the end of your line. This particularly applies on large lakes and reservoirs, where it is always worth while casting over rising fish, or in river grayling fishing, where shoals can sometimes be located by the presence of the odd rising fish, and the shoal can then be successfully fished with worm or grub.

Some comments on fishing methods

This book is not primarily about fishing methods and there is, in any event, a vast range of articles and books on tackle and technique for game fishing. What I wish to attempt is a few comments on fishing technique which stem fairly directly from my earlier consideration of the natural history of these fish.

Wet fly

Wet flies are, by definition, feathered lures fished below the surface. They can conveniently be divided into those which represent attempted imitations of a known food item, and those which do not – although there does seem to be a large vague area of fly dressings, such as wet sedge patterns (e.g. Pale Sedge), which may be construed by some as imitating something such as a hatching sedge, and fished by others as an unspecified lure. The following points about wet fly fishing seem relevant in a book of this sort and follow from our earlier discussion about food and feeding habits.

The well sunk lure There is little doubt that trout in many stillwaters respond well to large black flies or lures fished deeply by stripping in line after a very long cast. You do not need a shooting head to do this, although it clearly helps to work the fly over a longer distance. But you do need a fairly fast sinking line and perhaps a weighted fly. Anyone who intends doing much stillwater fishing is well advised, at least in present fishing conditions, to have two reels in his bag, one supplied with a floating line and the other with a fairly fast sinker. Many fishermen actually carry two rods with them to save the trouble of changing reels and threading lines, but that always seems to me pretty cumbersome. A coil of fine copper wire in one's pocket is a handy way of providing instant weight to a fly or lure, but of course many are dressed already weighted.

It is my impression that these flies or lures should be allowed to sink as near to the bottom as possible (it is interesting to note that this method of fishing is most popular in deepish lakes, heavily stocked, but lacking in natural weed and fly life), and then worked with a slow steady retrieve. Fish seem to be more attracted to a steady rate of retrieve than a slow/fast jerky one. Many of the fish take these lures with a tremendous bang, confirming my suspicion that they are not accepted in mistake for natural prey.

My own policy is to fish surface nymphs or dry flies by preference, but if they prove entirely unproductive, to choose a natural promontory over a deepish sheltered bay, put up my sinking line and a heavy black fly, and with the wind behind me, settle down for an hour's slog. That is about as much of it as I can take in the interest of filling the pot, but some other fishermen seem to become remarkably addicated to this method of fishing. There is no doubt that, in certain conditions, it can be very productive. I watched one man, soon after a small lake fishery had adopted a 'no limit' policy, remove from that water a staggering number of 1lb rainbows by this method. He maintained his position in one spot and was obviously benefiting from a shoal of rainbows, probably very recently introduced to the lake.

How many flies? In many waters fishing is invariably to one fly only, and when stripping a large fly or lure, no doubt more than one would make casting even more cumbersome than such fishing often is. (The long casting involved demands lack of bushes behind, aerialising a very long line, perhaps a shooting head line, and for the fastidious or naturally clumsy, a line tray.) But often wet fly fishing means fishing near to the surface, either from a boat on a lake or reservoir, from the bank in shallow weedy lake or loch, or downstream in a burn or river. In all these cases there is a question of whether a single fly is more or less advantageous than two, three, or in some lake fisheries in Scotland and Ireland, even four. In my view there is much to be said in favour of fishing two flies at a time, one fished as a dropper and one at the end of the leader. Such an arrangement permits one to work flies in two rather different styles at the same time, the end fly being drawn through the water in line or jerks, the dropper fly adopting a more up and down motion and, as one nears the end of the traverse with the cast, the dropper is either being worked in the surface film or actually coming in and out of the water. As is known to all those who have used the method, this can be a very effective manner of fishing, and on many occasions my entire bag of trout has been taken on the dropper fly. To those southern fellows who decry the northern practice of wet fly fishing with more than one fly on the cast, I would retort that it certainly does not result in dramatically increased catches. As for its being unsporting, the most murderous form of trout fishing in which I have indulged is fishing southern chalk streams with a large guinea-fowl hackled dry fly when trout are taking Green Drake mayflies. The Alexandra and Bloody Butcher, of savage fame, were never half so effective!

Fishing the nymph upstream As is now well recognised by most experienced fishermen, trout and grayling which are seen to be 'bulging', resulting in a pseudo-rise form or a minor disturbance of the water surface, are most frequently feeding on swimming nymphs. Such fish are often located just downstream of prolific weedbeds. Some stillwater fish taking midge pupae exhibit a similar rise form, although often, presumably because the pupae has reached the surface film, these fish produce a more authentic rise. Of course, some nymphing fish make no visible surface disturbance, and such fish may sometimes be detected in the clear water of a chalk stream by the sudden upwards or sideways thrust of the fish and sometimes by the show of white as the mouth opens. Detection is never easy, but it will be made easier by using good polaroid glasses (not simply smoked-glass sunglasses, which are useless).

Nymphing fish may be caught readily on sunken nymphs, using a floating line. There are three major problems involved. The first is delivering the fly so that it is at the correct depth when it approaches the fish; the second is to impart some movement to it to improve the resemblance to a swimming nymph; and the third is to detect the moment when the trout or grayling takes the nymph and strike accordingly.

I have no desire to write on this subject at great length. Other men of greater knowledge and skill than I have written many pages and books on the topic. But a few comments seem admissible. The first is a word of encouragement to the thousands of good fishermen who do not fish on chalk streams or other waters of extreme clarity. Many of the folk who have written on the topic give the impression that it is a method of very general application. Well, it is not. Taking the U.K. as a whole there are rather few waters in which a nymphing fish can be detected by sight one or two feet below the surface. So do not imagine that your eyesight is defective or your powers of observation deficient; even on chalk streams it is often very difficult. But this not to deny that fishing the nymph to bulging fish is very generally applicable. It is, and even on small streams trout may take swimming nymphs very readily and I have certainly caught many this way. On the other hand, on some of those streams fish seem less committed to nymphing and will often take a dry fly when it is presented to them, whereas nymphing trout on the Itchen ignore all dry flies whether natural or artificial.

Much has also been written on the 'induced take', that final wiggle of movement imparted to the sunk nymph when it is within the vision of the fish. Here again, although undeniably very effective, it is not, I think, very easy to do with delicacy, especially if you do not have a really good fix on the exact location of the fish. Moreover, it is often unnecessary, since I certainly hook the majority of my trout on sunken nymphs which are simply allowed to float down with the stream at the correct depth – I say 'with the stream' advisedly, since I think that on stillwaters the 'induced take' with the sunk nymph is a more crucial ingredient of success.

On getting the strike right I have nothing to add. I lose a lot of fish because I strike after the leader is seen to move and that is often too late. But a change of nymph will often bring another take in such circumstances, assuming the fish to be in a fixed feeding position or a stillwater cruiser.

My last comment on this topic is simply to stress that what I have written is equally applicable to grayling. These fish are reputed to remain on the bottom at all times, even when taking dry fly. That is not entirely true. I have frequently seen grayling nymphing 'on the fin' just a foot or so below the surface, and my observations are supported by other reports in the angling literature. Large grayling of over 1½lbs seem to rise to the dry fly on rather rare occasions but not infrequently they may be found feeding quite actively on sunken nymphs.

Fishing the nymph downstream Since casting downstream normally implies working one's flies against the current, I think it is much less certain that they are then taken in mistake for swimming nymphs – unless, that is, they happen to turn into very slack water. Working wet flies just below the surface is the fundamental method of fishing in many areas, especially fast streams and hill lochs. This is no doubt because in these situations the trout are hungry and will readily take any moving object as a potential food item. If one is fishing on slower, more productive rivers or streams, I think one has to become a little more subtle in the approach. One can do this by using a rather long line and lengthy leader – this to avoid being seen by the fish in the greater clarity of the slower clearer water – and letting the flies sink as they work round from 'across the river' where the cast commences its work. I frequently 'mend' my line when I am using this technique, in order to avoid dragging the leader and flies against the current. By letting out an extra foot of line now and again, one can keep the flies low in the water and simply let them hold their position in the slackish water where the eddies leave a quiet pocket behind stones or at the end of weedbeds. It is in these positions that I find I pick up most of my fish, whether brown trout in spring or grayling in autumn. There are, of course, many southern waters in which downstream fishing is expressly forbidden, and in any event the amount of weed in many chalk streams renders it a tricky technique in these situations.

I do actually have something of a bone to pick with the 'upstream only' pundits, and more especially with the 'upstream dry fly only' rule. A number of southern chalk streams hold many trout which rarely feed on surface fly. This is especially so on the Itchen, a river with which I am fairly familiar. Many large brown trout in this river seem to feed substantially on or near to the bottom and, even when nymphing in mid-water, can be very inaccessible to upstream flies. I feel that downstream wet fly fishing is rarely more productive than upstream on this sort of water, but in some situations it is the only method possible.

Dry fly

In favour of the dry fly Let me begin this section with a plea and an assurance. The plea is that, if you do not normally fish dry fly, you do so at the very next opportunity; the assurance, which goes with the plea, is that fishing dry fly is no more difficult than most wet fly or bait fishing and easier than both of these methods in many circumstances. There are still many fishermen whom I meet on rivers and reservoirs who have never experienced the particular pleasures of this method of fly fishing, which is a pity, since it has much to offer. Indeed, if I were to be limited to one type of fishing on all waters, this is the method which I would choose both in stillwater and river, and whether the quarry was sea trout, brown trout or grayling. For the truth is that, in reasonably experienced hands, dry fly fishing is quite frequently more productive of fish than any other type of game fishing. It is also very satisfying in that the direct placement of the fly, especially in a river situation, does require some skill, and appeals more to the spirit of the hunter in that the fisherman actually spots the fish (or more correctly, its rise) before attempting to catch it. I have fished dry fly on large rivers wading up to my waist, in tiny burns only a few feet from bank to bank, in mountain lochans, large reservoirs, and flooded gravel pits, and in all of these varied situations I find it a delightful and productive technique.

All you really need to begin practising dry fly fishing is a well balanced fly rod, a good floating line, a tapered cast, and a few dry flies anointed with some floatant oil. The pattern is unimportant at first – you will deceive trout in all sorts of situations with a dry Greenwell's Glory on a No. 14 or 16 hook. Whether on lake or river your first key task is to locate a feeding fish. This may take time and involve quite a lot of walking, but once found, you stand a good chance of catching him. If you aim to put the fly about a foot *above* the water surface, when it does settle it will land with great delicacy. The agonising excitement of watching one's dry fly float over a feeding fish must rank as one of the most rarified moments afforded to mere mortals. It is scarcely less thrilling on stillwater, since many lake trout feed by cruising in a distinct beat, so returning to the same spot every five minutes or so. As you see by the pattern of rises that a feeding fish is heading your way, it is all one can do to hold the rod still. All pretty electrifying. Especially when, with a satisfying slurp of water, your fly disappears into the maelstrom vortex which leads, somewhere in the centre, into the fish's mouth. The next moment you have no need to hold the rod still, for you are fastened tightly to an active and angry trout.

Of course, I have to admit that on some waters dry fly fishing remains, in the words of Brian Clarke, a minor tactic. After all, we do know that trout and grayling catch most of their prey well below the surface. But the enormous asset of fishing the dry fly is that one is fishing in the right place to a fish known to be on the feed. Even if you are pitching about in a boat on the choppy surface of Loch Leven, and your companion is patiently fishing the waves with his team of wet flies, if you see a rise or two amongst the wavelets, do not hesitate to knot on a dry fly. I have astonished many fishing friends by taking trout by this method even in a fast drifting boat and only a little surface activity. It does demand reasonably good eyesight to keep a sight of one's fly in such conditions, but the effort is amply repaid when the line is tightened into a fish. Some brave souls even advocate casting out a dry fly in the complete absence of surface rises, just in the hope of attracting a passing fish. I must admit to having tried this dodge on a few occasions but very rarely have I found it to be successful. If a fish does finally come up, my concentration will by then have wandered to some other interesting topic (such as the proof of Pythagoras's theorem, or the thought of a pint at the local hostelry) and the fly will have slipped from my conscious gaze. When I finally come to my senses and strike, the fish is long since gone elsewhere to ponder in peace on the curiosities of the artificial fly.

Dry fly fishing for grayling can be very effective, although I have to admit that the larger grayling fall more readily to other methods of fishing. But in the autumn months my catch with the dry fly normally compares very favourably with that of other anglers wielding wet flies or trotting a maggot. On the question of fish size, I also fancy that, where trout are concerned, the dry fly man's basket contains heavier fish than that of his wet fly companion. In other words, small trout feed less frequently on surface food than their larger brethren: a situation directly opposite to the grayling one.

What the fish actually sees When using sunken flies there is little scope for argument about what the fish actually sees. Wet flies and lures must be visualised much as we see them, with some allowance made for the movement of the hackles in the working of the fly through the water. But with dry flies the question is much more open. I have spent many interesting hours looking at dry flies on water surfaces, in situations ranging from beer mugs, through perspex casserole dishes and glass aquaria, to the river itself – the latter most frequently with the aid of a camera and a friendly subaqua enthusiast. The upshot of all this peering and photographing (see *Fig. 2.7*) is the conclusion that, by and large, the fish sees something very different from the alluring concoctions and confections which adorn the display cabinets of tackle dealers and, in lesser numbers, our own fly boxes.

The most dramatic conclusion is that, particularly when flies are knotted to a leader and anointed with floatant, they float *hook down*, which means that the most striking first impression of an artificial dry fly from the fish's angle is a hook. Normally the hook hangs down from the surface at some angle, but terrible in its nakedness and barbed menace. Since very few flies have an abdomen which, even on a New Year's morning (I speak as a Scot) closely resembles a barbed hook, anything we can do to alter that impression and hide the hook in the hackle is bound to improve the authenticity of our imitations.

The second conclusion is that, when you place the natural and artificial together on the water surface and view from below, almost all our artificials are seen to be much too big and heavy. They lack the delicacy of the real thing. Now I know that if you leave the hackle off a dry fly the blessed thing will not float, but I do think that the amount of hackle and its length can often be greatly reduced. Even clipping the hackle short with scissors may reduce the apparent sophistication of the final creation – we ourselves have been so brainwashed, or 'conditioned' as the psychologists and behaviourists call it, that we have an ideal fly in our mind's eye which probably bears little relation to any flying insect, but satisfies certain artistic and technical demands about the turn of the feather, the rake of the tail whisks and the finish of the head – but such clipping does reduce the size of the fly and helps to retain plenty of short hackle near to the body, assisting floatation.

My reaction to the problem of authentic appearance is that I never bother to tie winged flies; I use very lightly hackled flies, and rarely do I use anything larger than a No. 16 hook. I am convinced that the greatest disincentive which we can offer to a trout or grayling when we present our dry fly for inspection is its sheer size. If you try, as I have done many times, answering repeated refusals with a reduction in size, you will very frequently find that your fly is finally taken. Now I know that small flies must be tied on small hooks and that these may bring some penalty of lost fish. But for me, better to have hooked and lost than never to have hooked at all! So do not be put off small hooks and flies. You will catch more fish with them in the long run, not less.

A more general inference emerges from any serious study of the appearance, from below the water surface, of natural and artificial flies, and it is one which ought to have very profound effects on our philosophy of dry fly angling. The inference is this. *That the duns of say medium olive, iron blue, and even march brown resemble one another much more closely than they do the artificial pattern of any one of them.* I am convinced that this conclusion is inescapable for anyone who has taken the trouble to do the necessary experiment. Its effects on our fishing philosophy should be, I think, that we be less concerned about what our artificial flies are called, but more concerned about whether their general size and appearance make them fly-like. I think we should be much less concerned about precise colours of hackles, wings and bodies, let alone whether the wings are correctly cocked or set, and more concerned about hiding the hook and generally representing an ephemeropteran dun or a sedge (if that is what we are trying to imitate). For let us admit, there is plenty of room for improvement in our attempts at fly imitation and it is our good fortune that in reality the game fish which we pursue are less discriminating in their choice of fly than common legend admits.

Dapping Certain Irish loughs are world famous as localities where large sea trout may be caught by dapping. Long rods are used from boats, and light lines of silk or monofilament (generally the former), to which are attached haystacks of hackle which are popularly supposed to imitate craneflies. Natural craneflies are themselves sometimes used. The wind is used to carry out the long line and the large fly is simply allowed to settle on and lift off the water surface 'with the wind'. Now I have never dapped for sea trout – sadly – but it sounds an exciting sport. I have dapped for both brown trout and char with some success, using monofilament line. It is tricky to use and easily becomes tangled, but with a reasonably stiff breeze one can work a fly out a very long way. I have found dapping useful when I have been shore fishing on a lake or loch in a reasonable wind and either found conventional casting too arduous or else failed to reach some obviously rising fish. So, even for those of you never privileged to fish for an Irish sea trout, do not forget the possibility of dapping. Incidentally, one of the obvious reasons for the use of 'haystacks' is not that the fish necessarily prefer them, but that they remain in sight at the end of a long line. It is certainly a rather important point. No use dapping a No. 18 Iron Blue!

Bait fishing

Many people turn up their brandy-stained noses at the mention of bait fishing. That, for me, is a very mistaken point of view. I concede that worm fishing in a flooded river can, at times, be a very easy way to fill the bag, but the same criticism can be levelled at every other type of fishing in certain circumstances. Given the right situation every fishing tactic can yield a large basket but, fortunately for the sport, these occasions make rare entries in our diaries. What is so crassly ignorant about the attitude of the anti-bait brigade is that catching fish by means of upstream clear water worming, or, in many conditions, by downstream long trotting with worm or maggots, demands very considerable knowledge and skill. My personal position is that while I feel reasonably competent with a dry fly, I am far from an adequate mastery of the art of long trotting, and am often envious of the obvious skill displayed by some other men in this aspect of the game.

Surface flies The use of natural dry flies as bait falls between two stools, being 'infra-dig' to the fly fishermen and a bit specialised for most convinced bait fishermen. Indeed the only situation in which it seems to be practised with complete dignity is when natural craneflies (daddy-long-legs) are sometimes tied to a small hook and used for dapping on Irish loughs. Now with all due respect (which phrase, curiously, commonly implies with no respect at all!) to those with such views, I think this attitude unfortunate and a trifle stuffy. Quite a few situations have come my way in which trout were almost uncatchable by conventional methods but could be caught in this way. I think that one of the special features of using the natural fly is that fish will take them even if they are floated down to them from upstream, that is, with some drag often imparted to the fly.

Much of my fishing apprenticeship was served on the Edinburgh Water of Leith, even then grossly over-fished and under-stocked. In a word, it was 'difficult' fishing. It was rare to find a fish feeding in an easy catchable location, but I did discover by dint of quiet observation (what we schoolboys lacked in experience and equipment we could partially balance with the extra time afforded by school hours – it was trout fishing versus the horrors of Latin homework) that a few trout fed exclusively in certain whirlpools. These were large and quite slow circular eddies, the best of which was formed by the entry of a tributary called the Murray Burn. On the surface of these whirlpools lay a mass of foam, partly the result of turbulence, but part also, I fear, an early token of pollution by paper mills which lay some miles upstream. In any event, some trout had discovered that the underside of the mass of foam held many insects, and there they fed, making tiny almost undetectable blips in the foam when they sucked in an insect. My first attempts to catch such fish were with dry flies but these proved quite unrewarding, and that for a few reasons. Firstly, my dry flies invariably sank in the foam, apparently because it acted like a detergent froth, removing the oily covering from the fly and making it quickly wet. Secondly, I could not readily follow the movement of the fly round the pool because it was lost to sight under the foam, and, thirdly, many of the feeding rises of the fish were so small that it was always an open question whether one was imagining the whole thing. The fish themselves were entirely invisible.

Finally, in desperation, I determined to try a live bluebottle. Easier said than done, finding a bluebottle, but finally I arrived at the water with my tackle and one or two bluebottles in a matchbox. Rather than trying to impale the unfortunate insect on the hook, I tied it on with thread, and that is an approach I would also recommend to any other enterprising angler tempted to try his hand at live-flying! Finally, I dropped my bluebottle, still struggling, on to the surface of the whirlpool. Now here again was a bonus, for fishing in such conditions does not demand any true casting, and a live fly tied to a hook is scarcely castable. My struggling fly finally disappeared amidst the foam, but only seconds later a miniature eruption in the foam brought a reflex strike from me and I was tight into a trout. That fish had obviously been as eager for the bluebottle, after a strict diet of greenfly and midges, as are the spring cattle for the new grass after a winter diet of mouldy hay. Landing that fish was not easy either, for a net was not numbered amongst my possessions at that time, so fish had to be played out and 'beached' or lifted out by hand. I had a small circle of spectators by the time I lifted out that fine fish from the whirlpool, all of ¾lb and a largish fish for those waters. It proved to be the first of many, for, as I searched the river for miles around, I came on other whirlpools, none quite as productive as the first, but often with a resident trout with a healthy preference for live bluebottles. I hope that my anti-bait friends will not judge too harshly these youthful rewards of an inexperienced but enterprising angler.

A similar tale from my library of fishing memories concerns the use of a natural mayfly for the destruction of a chalk stream trout. This particular chalk stream had few of the restrictions of the classier stretches, but held a few good trout. One of about 3lbs lived in an uncatchable situation under a hawthorn bush and I would defy any grand master of casting technique to have put a fly anywhere near to that fish. In the day in question I was on the same bank as the fish and its protecting shrubbery. Peering through the branches, I could see that my friend was feeding regularly and on that day it seemed that all other fish in the river had gone off on holiday. I sat down on the bank to eat a sandwich and watch the swallows and martins hawking for flies, and as I pondered awhile, became aware that the odd mayfly dun was around. In the recesses of my mind there took shape the notion that I might, I just might, tempt my friend under the hawthorn with a live mayfly floated from above so that it would go in under the branches. I had tried a similar dodge once or twice with an artificial dry fly, but always the drag put down the fish. As with the bluebottle, finding a live mayfly was more easily conceived than executed and, when caught, it turned out to be a darn sight more difficult to tie on to the hook. But finally I succeeded in dropping a somewhat sad mayfly plus hook (and a tiny one it had to be) on to the current and let it find its way in under the hawthorn. One or two attempts were necessary to steer it into the appropriate spot, but finally my floating livebait came within sight of my fishy friend. The response was never in question. He was on to it like a tornado and whenever he felt the hook, dived into the recesses of the deep hole which lay under that tree. My small hook stood little chance of holding, and I was left with a hook impaled in the branches of the hawthorn and some disappointment in my heart. But I was not to be outdone. The next weekend I was back with another mayfly and a little more mental preparation for what was to follow. He took as eagerly as before but this time, whenever the hook was safely home, I slackened off and let him sulk a bit at the bottom of the hole. As you can imagine, a heavy fish in a deep hole and strong water, downstream and under a tree, all adds up to a delicate situation. But this time I hung on and played a careful waiting game, tiring him more by bewilderment than force. It all ended well for me, for I finally netted out a tired brown trout of just under 3lbs, taken on the live mayfly! In over-fished waters with very few fish available, such an occasion is a rare and splendid achievement.

I hope my two little tales will help to convince at least some of my readers that there is a place in the repertoire of the enthusiastic trout fishermen for the use of the live fly. May you live to have similar tales to tell and memories to cherish. It is obvious that many important items of surface food are too small to be satisfactorily attached to a hook, but small beetles and grasshoppers are other examples which may be added to the ones already mentioned; mayfly, bluebottle and cranefly. So, if all else fails and you are game to experiment, all you need is a roll of fine thread, some small hooks, and enough athleticism to catch the necessary insects.

Worms and maggots

Catching and keeping the bait Earthworms of many different species are used as bait by fishermen. The large garden worm, *Lumbricus*, is generally too large for anything but fishing a flooded river, but many smaller species are suitable. Particular favourites are two small worms which are closely related, one *Eisenia rosea*, which is bright pink in colour with an orange band (this is the saddle or clitellum possessed by many worms), and the other somewhat darker, but with clear orange rings between many segments, is called *Eisenia foetida*. The first is, I think, the worm which is commonly known as the 'gilt-tail' in the midlands, and the second is generally referred to as the 'brandling'. Both are common in compost heaps and dung middens, but the *Lumbricus* favours the midden or the well-rotted compost, while *Eisenia rosea* is commonest in grass compost and incompletely rotted manure heaps. Those of us who have gardens may easily guarantee ourselves an ample supply of both species by conserving leaf mould or grass clippings and allowing them to rot steadily. When collecting the worms, they are best placed in a large tobacco tin with some dry moss, but be sure to puncture the lid with a few holes. Worms quickly die from lack of air.

The maggots which we buy are the larvae of the bluebottle or blowfly, *Calliphora*, and they are normally bought mixed with fine sawdust. Again, they must be kept in a container with air holes, and should not be allowed to become too warm. If the larvae become warm or dry, they will either die or pupate, and neither state is of any use to the angler. A domestic refrigerator at about 5°C. provides an excellent temperature if you wish to keep your beef maggots for a few days, but your family may not take kindly to the idea of finding tins of maggots in the fridge! If your maggots do pupate, tip them on a fire or you will hatch out a large crop of bluebottles some days later.

Other 'maggots' which may be used as bait include wasp larvae (if you happen to be clearing out a wasps' nest), caddis fly larvae removed from their cases, and 'docken grubs', which are the larvae of the ghost moth and may be dug up from around the roots of dock plants or dandelions. All of these grubs tend to be softer than maggots and I cannot believe that they offer any special advantage to the angler in reward for the labour of obtaining them.

Using the bait – clear water worming This method of bait fishing has been used for many years in rivers of the Scottish border country, and they are well suited to it. What one wants is a smallish stream which is fordable, so that one can fish from either bank as necessary, with pools and glides sheltered by bushes or undercut banks, these latter for the concealment of the angler. The technique involves throwing the bait upstream with a cross between a flick and a roll cast, landing it at the head of a pool or glide. A long rod is necessary to permit easy and gentle presentation of the bait and allow the angler to keep a discreet distance downstream. This method of fishing is probably best accomplished with a long fly rod fitted with fly reel, floating line and a long leader of 10 feet or so. Small hooks seem to be best, nothing bigger than a 14 and probably smaller.

Now I cannot pretend to be a great expert at this method of fishing, but I do find it very satisfying to practise. It can be used for both trout and grayling and, with good cover, can prove rewarding in even low water conditions and on a bright day. Few greater challenges exist for the angler than creeping up with extreme stealth on a trout which is located in clear shallow water, and successfully presenting a worm or maggot to that fish without disturbance. The brandling is the favourite bait, and some border anglers favour a 'Stewart' tackle of two hooks tied to gut in tandem. Although I have never actually used them in this situation, I feel sure that beef maggots would be equally effective.

Long trotting This method of bait fishing is almost never used for trout, but is widely favoured by grayling anglers fishing on largish rivers in winter. Either maggots or small worms are used, some fishermen swearing by one, some by another. I slightly favour the worm but I cannot claim to have carried out a rigorous comparison between the two baits. The tackle is a long light bait rod, probably fibreglass, a fine nylon monofilament line and either a centre pin or fixed spool reel. Again, anglers argue over the choice of reel. From my observation I have the impression that the centre pin is much the better reel for this method of fishing, but I invariably use a fixed spool since I have never acquired the other. The tackle is made up with a largish easily cocked float and enough shot to keep the bait on or near to the bottom, and, having found a stance at the head of a likely run or pool, one allows the bait to search out the bottom as the float works its way down the pool. Bites may be very gentle, and much of the skill is distinguishing between the hesitancy of the float which indicates a true bite, and that which simply results from weed or stones on the bottom. Finding the fish when they are in a mood to feed is what this game is all about. I think that you should change your maggot frequently, since smell is probably involved in the fish finding and taking these baits. Some anglers also like to colour their maggots and claim to catch more fish. Maybe it is an additional releaser! You can catch twenty grayling in half-an-hour with skill and good fortune (I never have, so do not be disheartened), but you must be prepared to search for the fish. Some men adopt the policy of taking up station at a good pool and continuing to fish with dogged persistence in the hope that the fish will come on the feed. Generous handfuls of maggots are often thrown into the water as encouragement. Being of a restless temperament, I favour the roving method and so go from pool to pool until I locate some feeding fish. Which is better I will never know for certain, but I am convinced that once the cold weather of winter has come, the grayling may forsake some of their favourite water, and finding their current location is never easy. An excellent account of this method of fishing is to be found in Righyni's book *The Grayling*.

All I can do is to give you the benefit of my comparative inexperience. I find that worms are better than maggots as bait; that fishing as near to the bottom as possible is advantageous; that a small hook baited with one small worm or single maggot is best; and that fishing slack water in the middle of two currents in a river, provided it is fairly deep, is often very good. But I have many blank days to admit to, as well as some very happy memories, so I certainly cannot claim to be invariably successful.

Creeper fishing The larvae of the stonefly, locally known in the border country as 'the creeper', is a popular bait in that area. I have never tried this method so I list it here not out of knowledge but simply because it no doubt deserves mention. The creeper is fished after the manner of the clear water worm, I believe, and is probably very effective in rivers where it is common.

Spinning

This form of fishing involves the use of a fast take-up reel, most frequently of a fixed spool type, to accomplish rapid retrieval of a bait, the bait having a spinning action imparted to it by fins or other rotary devices. To my knowledge, spinning is never employed by intention to catch grayling, only trout, and for the latter it is used in lakes, rivers and in the sea. (Salmon fishers who use a small 'Meps' spoon early in the season often hook grayling on these lines.) Some anglers advocate the use of dead minnow baits for the capture of trout in large rivers, the minnow being fished in a sink and draw fashion. It is arguable whether this approach should be termed spinning since the bait does not necessarily spin, although a spinning reel is frequently used. But whether it should be properly discussed under bait fishing or spinning scarcely matters, since it is not a method I have tried and do not propose to discuss further.

Spinning is often regarded by those who have never tried it as a wicked and murderous way of killing trout, but in truth it is much less productive than these people seem to suppose. On the rivers and lakes where spinning for trout is permitted I have watched the method many times when I have been employed in fly fishing, and on numerous occasions I have also used it myself. If I were asked to choose between fly and spinning in terms of potential productivity, I would almost invariably choose fly fishing. Spinning can be very boring, especially in large lakes and reservoirs, although on rivers it can prove more interesting and more difficult. But it does seem to me that there is nothing to choose between spinning a small minnow or spoon and stripping a large lure, as far as stillwater angling goes. On large stillwater fisheries where the trout population per cubic yard of water is low and the popularity index is hovering dangerously near to the break-even line, I would advocate the permitted use of spinning for trial periods. Vast baskets would rarely result, I believe, but some died-in-the-wool spinning men would be attracted to try their hand. Some might even be seduced to convert occasionally to a fly rod.

I have had wide experience over a number of years of fishing small Scottish hill lochs in the highlands and islands of Scotland. Most holidaymakers imagine that trout fishing on all such waters is free, a belief which is almost invariably untrue, but remains unchallenged because of the shortage of bailiffs to keeper the water. So it is that, while fly fishing, I often find that a party of half a dozen chaps appears over the hill, as if from nowhere, but in fact emanating from luggage-laden cars perched just out of sight and still bulging with wives, children, dogs and the odd sailing dinghy. These newcomers will invariably ignore me, assuming me to be one of the notoriously taciturn natives, but proceed to unship spinning rods and reels and send a multitude of diverse items of ironmongery in arcs of varying geometry over the placid waters. At this point it is my custom to reel in my line and flies, light my pipe to keep away the midges, and patiently observe my companions. Their stay rarely exceeds thirty minutes and it is extremely unusual for them to have netted any fish in that time (the word netted is somewhat inappropriate, for they will very infrequently possess a net between them). With obvious disillusionment and frustration at the midges and the dearth of fish, my companions depart as speedily as they came and calm will descend once more.

Now to be fair, I have not painted spinning for trout in its best colours, and many skilled and dedicated fishermen use this method on various waters. But my story, which must be familiar to many of you, is primarily intended to drive home the point that spinning is often, indeed most frequently, rather unproductive, even when fish are quite numerous. The small trout which struggle for survival in small highland lochans are not the most fastidious of fish, but even they cannot be indiscriminately hauled from the water at the glance of a devon minnow.

Harking back to the arguments advanced in Chapter 7, I am not of the opinion that trout take spun lures in mistake for food, but rather out of curiosity or aggression. This is nowhere better illustrated than in a river with some large fast pools. If one allows a small devon to remain rotating at high speed in the strong current, not infrequently a trout will come and slash at the lure, often without connecting to the hooks. No natural prey ever behaves, or could behave, in this extraordinary fashion, yet somehow this action of the spinning lure angers or stimulates the trout to make a rapid grab at the object in question.

Having advocated spinning for trout to be permitted on some large stillwaters such as Rutland or Chew, or more especially on waters where boats are not available, I would like to emphasise that I think the presentation of a small weighted spinning device by the aid of monofilament and a fixed spool reel much more sensible than the currently accepted technique which demands fast sink lines with shooting heads, weighted but non-spinning lures, probably a line tray, and a quite unreasonable amount of wading. Such deep and distant fishing could far more effectively be executed by the use of some simple spinning equipment and shoes instead of waders.

A more interesting aspect of trout spinning can be found in river fishing, although again, you should not expect to empty the river. You will need to use a smallish minnow or a small 'Meps' spoon, and probably to do a deal of stealthy wading, fishing down and across (although some experienced fishers use it up and across) and investigating all the holes and reaches of the water, especially under banks and overhanging trees. I find that it pays to fish the minnow or spoon as slowly as possible consistent with the need to keep it off the bottom, and herein lies much of the skill, for weeds and sunken branches pose a constant problem for the trout spinner. If you have no other, your fly rod can be pressed into service for this task, but if it is a precious rod you would be well advised to save the obvious strain on the top joint and use a properly designed spinning rod of short length and stiffish action. You must also realise that the fish you are now pursuing will probably be a separate trout population from the ones which you stalk with tapered leader and fly. This implies not only that you may find much of your usual fly water unsuitable for spinning, but also that you will want to concentrate on deep holes and quiet deeps which, in your fly fishing experience, are quite unproductive. You may be surprised what can be extricated from stretches of water regarded by fly men as fishless – not only branches and old boots, but the occasional good fish as well.

This is an aspect of the craft which I think we must constantly stress in the hearing of our fly-only brethren: that spinning for river trout often complements rather than competes with fly fishing, permitting, as it does, the taking of fish which would otherwise prove beyond our angling reach.

Spinning for sea trout One of the most exciting forms of fishing known to mere mortals is surely the taking of estuarine sea trout by spinning. Its excitement owes much to the time and place, for often it is best near to nightfall, when the tide is beginning to flood up between the banks of seaweed, sending the oystercatchers on to new mud banks and tempting the silvery sea trout to come nosing and splashing their way into the river estuaries. Unfortunately rather few of us happen to be in such suitable localities in the productive months of September and October, and in most years I have only the odd day at the end of August to refer to, when the true sea trout run has scarce begun and the tales of the native fishermen of large baskets and giant fish have to be shrugged off with a certain hopeless envy. Certainly large fresh run sea trout are the most magnificent expression of *Salmo fario* imaginable, and give just cause for the early anglers to honour it with the status of a distinct species.

So, as one who is familiar with many good sea trout waters in Skye and the Outer Hebrides, but, enviously, less familiar than I would like to be with the fine fish which inhabit them, let me share with you what I can glean from my memories. First, some perhaps rather obvious but, I think, sound advice. Use a stout rod, heavy monofilament and two swivels: seaweed and rocks can make heavy demands on tackle. Gumboots or waders are essential, as is a good knowledge of the estuary you intend to fish. Make sure you know what the estuary looks like at low water and at high tide – they are of course very different, but an educated imagination when fishing demands an acquaintance with both situations. The beginning of a flood tide at about dusk seems to be the ideal time to fish and so tide tables and local knowledge must be consulted beforehand. I would recommend taking up a stance on a promontory known to be safe at high tide (and known to permit good access to the shore at high tide!), and doing all one's fishing, if possible, from this one point. But in some estuaries a lot of movement is possible and indeed desirable. The sea trout may well make their presence known by rising and jumping, but beware the former, for shoals of mullet also favour estuaries and their rises can look deceptively like those of sea trout. A small minnow or a small 'Meps' spoon seems the best lure and you may have to retrieve your device very frequently to remove strands of seaweed. If you get stuck in the seaweed, a very strong pull is necessary to free the hooks – hence the strong line required – but make sure you are not facing the weed when exerting full pressure. A treble of hooks in the cheek may put a stop to more than one evening after the sea trout. Another tip is not to try biting through nylon trace with teeth when sea fishing, partly because it is pretty tough, but more because, if you have dragged it through jelly fish tentacles (and in the West Highlands you are bound to do that every few minutes) the trace will be coated with stinging cells. These will not penetrate your skin, but can easily penetrate the soft tissue of the inside of your mouth. With jelly fish, as with many other experiences, once bitten, twice shy!

If you get hooked on the sport (as well as the fish, I hope), I would recommend the book *Sea Trout Fishing* by Jock Scott for an authoritative discussion of this and other aspects of sea trout fishing.

Trolling for large lake trout Some fishing books contain graphic accounts of giant brown trout, oft times referred to as 'ferox' trout, which have been extricated from certain deep lakes and lochs by the trolling of a large minnow at great depth (see discussion in Chapter 6 and *Fig. 6.3*). This occupation requires a boat and considerable patience and is added here only for the record. I doubt very much whether any trout, of whatever gargantuan dimensions, choose to live for even the main part of their lives at the depths fished by such methods. As someone cleverly remarked in another connection, it may be worth doing, but it's not worth going to do!

Is it cruel?

All fishermen are asked and ask themselves this question on many occasions. Can I interest you in my answer? As a biologist this is a question which I face regularly in other contexts, both with wild and laboratory animals ranging from earthworms to chimpanzees. Almost all professional biologists would agree with me in saying that one has to assess cruelty and suffering of animals on a sliding scale, depending on the sophistication of their nervous systems. Few of us worry very deeply about cruelty to slugs, limpets or houseflies (all invertebrates) but most of us are deeply concerned about cruelty to horses or deer (which are of course mammals). Let me remind you of the probable order of precedence in our sliding scale of faunistic sophistication.

Animals without backbones i.e. invertebrates	1.	Amoeba – Single celled microscopic animals
	2.	Sea anemones and jelly fishes – Coelenterata
	3.	Worms and leeches – Annelida
	4.	Insects and crustaceans – Arthropoda
	5.	Snails and octopuses – Mollusca
Animals with backbones i.e. vertebrates	6.	Fishes
	7.	Amphibians
	8.	Reptiles
	9.	Birds
	10.	Mammals

In this table I have included only a few of the many groups of invertebrates, but all the vertebrate groupings are given. You will see that fish are the lowest and least sophisticated of all vertebrates, and studies on their structure and behaviour confirm this. Therefore, although it is clearly not pleasurable or even painless for a fish to be impaled on a hook for a few minutes, it is silly to attempt to correlate such a situation with impaling a mammal on a hook. Simple observation confirms what we should accept – that recently hooked fish often return to normal feeding behaviour within minutes of their return to the water. So in my view the temporary impaling of a fish on a hook is perhaps equivalent to enclosing a tadpole in a jam jar, netting birds for ringing purposes, or startling a deer when we walk through the woods – all experiences which the animal might happily do without, but none in any meaningful sense, cruel. Pointless laboratory experiments involving stress – induction in rats and dogs – seems to me to be cruel, as indeed are gin traps whether used for foxes, rabbits or rats. The assault on a whale with an explosive harpoon seems to me incredibly barbaric considering the fact that whales are mammals of an intellectual sophistication very close to our own. But then, do not we highly sophisticated and civilised humans use bombs and napalm?

So be gentle and courteous to your fish, but not over-sentimental. If they do not end up in your frying pan they may provide a satisfying meal for an otter or a mink. For the average fish, not a happy thought either way!

10

Some Thoughts on Hatcheries and Fisheries

Without doubt the most dramatic development in game fishing over the last fifty years has been the progressive widespread production of trout in essentially artificial conditions. This revolutionary change has not only rendered trout a relatively cheap table fish but has made artificial stocking of angling waters the essential ingredient in the sport of almost all game fishermen. Without such stocking most of our angling waters would cease to be productive fisheries within the year.

I would therefore like to round off this book with a few thoughts on this astonishing development, its threats, its promises, its techniques and its benefits. But in doing so I must emphasise that I am neither a professional fish biologist nor a fish farmer, so my comments are essentially amateur. But I have visited many fish farms specialising both in table and sport production, and have been an interested observer as biologist, fisherman, and one-time agriculturalist. The large-scale production of trout is actually not so different from some other methods of intensive stock farming and indeed many of the economic and management principles seem to be essentially the same. We would do well to remember as responsible anglers that the benefits of trout production which we now enjoy are inextricably linked up with the ethical and environmental problems of intensive farming.

Hatcheries

In the economics of trout production it often seems to be advantageous to separate the production of young fish from the production of edible or stockable fish. Hatcheries specialise in hatching trout eggs and producing fingerlings. As we have already discussed, fertilisation of trout ova with milt is easily accomplished by stripping hen and cock fish. Hatching the eggs is somewhat more arduous. The crucial element is the presence of a good supply of clean silt-free water, at a constant temperature somewhere between 7 and 12°C., and free from undesirable impurities. Such water is not easy to come by, the ideal being spring water from underground artesian wells. Drinking water in most districts is too highly chlorinated to be useful, and in any event the amounts required would be expensive as a metered supply.

During incubation the fertile eggs are kept in trays with a constant current of water passing over them, and dead eggs are removed regularly since they form a site for fungal infection which may spread also to the living eggs. Some keepers also use a constant drip of Malachite to deter fungal growth. When the eggs hatch the alevins feed on their yolk sacs, but once they have used up that store, they need to be fed. A much favoured food is the so-called 'eggs' of Artemia, the fairy shrimp. This is a small swimming crustacean, and actually the 'eggs' are dormant embryos which 'hatch' shortly after being added to water. The tiny larvae which appear swim with a bobbing movement like water fleas and make ideal food for the tiny fish. Nowadays, however, almost all hatcheries feed fry on special high protein fry food made up in tiny pellets. Hatcheries normally sell both fertile eggs and fingerling fish, and the former are now transported by air all over the world.

Trout farms

Although many trout farms strip their own fish and hatch their own eggs, many others simply buy in fingerling fish and rear these on in stew ponds. Large farms may have ten or twenty separate stew ponds, many with fish of differing ages, and a constant flow of good water running through the entire interconnected system. Trout farming is not as easy as it sounds.

Many parasitic and other diseases are serious problems in trout farms, and high densities of fish favour the rapid spread of disease. Unless the farms are exceptionally favourably situated, they also tend to be at the mercy of the water flow in an adjoining river, which may be dangerously low in summer – artificial water aeration is customary – and high in winter. Sudden floods are one of the worst hazards, and not a few fish farmers have lost their entire stock in one momentous overnight flood. Another constant threat to the fish farmer is poaching, not of the odd fish, but of hundreds of fish, often carried out by gangs of rather nasty characters. If you know of the whereabouts of a fish farm, do not wander uninvited just to have a look – it is probably booby-trapped and equipped with a secret alarm system, if not protected by Alsatian guard dogs! Sadly, it all seems to be justified and such measures still do not entirely prevent occasional large-scale losses. Natural predators are less troublesome, but mink, herons and cormorants can all cause occasional problems.

If the farm is marketing fish only for the table, then they will be harvested at about ½lb in weight and will probably be exclusively rainbow; if partly or wholly for stocking, they may be grown on to various sizes, some rainbows being grown for stocking up to 6lbs in weight. Browns grow more slowly and are more expensive to rear than rainbows on a weight-for-weight basis. Small farms may simply hand feed the fish on special pelleted food once or twice a day, but large farms normally utilise mechanical feeders, many of which release pellets when a bar is knocked or agitated by the fish, thus avoiding wastage of food. It is interesting to remark that the ability of trout to use such feeders is an example of learned reflex behaviour (see Chapter 7). The economy of trout farms is very dependent on the price of pellet food.

But, as with many other innovations and developments in modern society, trout farming brings problems and disadvantages along with its obvious benefits. Most of these arise from the connection of the farm to the flow system of a river, with consequent re-entry into the river of water which has passed through the stew ponds. Various pollution problems occur, arising from the fact that the water is low in oxygen and often rich in nitrogenous waste from fish excrements and uneaten trout food. If a stretch of river supports a number of ancillary farms, the main water may become toxic to fish and any existing river fishery ruined. I gather this unhappy state of affairs is not uncommon in Scandinavia, but I do not know how frequent it is in the U.K. Fish parasites and disease organisms may also be shed in large numbers from trout farms into neighbouring rivers, causing death and disease amongst wild fish, and of course the fish themselves may escape and prove, in the views of at least some fishermen, an undesirable addition or replacement of an existing trout population.

Transporting live fish

Compared with many coarse fish, trout are good travellers. To help them to survive well on a long road journey they are commonly transported in special trailers with either cooling facilities or, more commonly, a continuous bubbled supply of oxygen or compressed air. On the other hand grayling are very poor travellers, and die quickly in the limited confines of a 50- or 100-gallon tank. Various measures are used to facilitate their transport besides cooling or aeration of the water. One method which is frequently adopted is to anaesthetise the fish with a water soluble anaesthetic termed MS222, marketed by Sandoz Chemicals. This seems to cause the fish no permanent harm but reduces their respiration very considerably and they seem to travel in a much better state. Some farmers also bubble oxygen into the water before attempting to transport coarse fish, and this measure might also be of benefit in transporting grayling. Small grayling also seem to travel much more readily than large ones.

Fishery management

We are all, as fishermen, at the receiving end of fishery management policy when we wield our rods and flies, but it is perhaps useful to take an objective look at fishery management from the point of view of owner as well as customer. Most fisheries are run with the aim of making a profit and with stock fish costing up to £1 per pound for rainbow, and sometimes double that figure for brown trout, it is abundantly clear that no one paying, say £5 a day, should take on average more than about £2's worth of fish, allowing a figure of about £2 per angler per day for the cost of overheads.

The overheads which we are talking about are very largely tied up with the labour necessary for the maintenance of security, weed cutting, maintenance of banks and roads, and the general culture of the fish. The latter may involve netting out undesirable fish species, careful monitoring of existing stock, and the maintenance and encouragement of natural food for the fish. It seems to me that one of the tendencies of many fisheries which run on a so-called 'put-and-take' principle is to greatly over-stock the water and neglect the propagation of desirable weed growth and the invertebrate animal life which goes with it. This may produce hungry, easily caught, fish but in the long run it must lead to a type of fishing which is increasingly boring and unnatural. However delighted we may be when we first land a 5lb rainbow, our pleasure is hardly enhanced by the discovery that the same fish was reared in a stew pond and introduced to the fishery only days before its capture. I certainly find immensely more satisfaction in catching fish which, if not truly wild, at least seem to have become part of the natural fauna of the lake or river from which I have taken them.

May I now grind one of the axes in my armoury? It concerns weed growth. It seems to me that, especially on rivers, but also partly on lakes, many keepers cut the weed too drastically, often aiming for only two cuts in the year. Just as two visits per year to the hairdresser may lead to an over-dramatic removal of hair, so two cuts of weed often results in very close shaving indeed. Not only is much of the valuable fish food removed with the weed, but the desperate fish are left with nowhere to hide and may travel a long way up or down stream in order to find cover. I have known streams denuded in this way to lose their fish population virtually overnight, and fish may be very slow to return. So, in my view, 'little and often' should be the policy for good weed control, though how that principle fits in with the economy of fishery management I am not sure. Much the same rule applies to the introduction of new stock fish. Sadly, even in very large fisheries, it seems to be very difficult to organise the constant introduction of small numbers of new fish. Most frequently they are added from one or two convenient sites, many hundreds at a time, and most seem to be removed from the immediate neighbourhood within hours or days of introduction. Let us pray for the increase of fisheries, both river and stillwater, which can rely very considerably on growing-on fish introduced at the ½lb size or less, with the introduction of a few really large fish at regular intervals serving to top up an existing semi-wild population.

While I am grinding axes, let me also say something about the size of fish stocked or caught. I think that a good healthy fish of 1¼–1½lbs is an ideal size, both for catching and eating. While the presence of a few really large fish, wild and 'tame', adds great spice and excitement to any fishery, I think it is wasteful of resources to use fish of 2–3lbs as standard stock fish. Most anglers will be very content with less. On the other hand, heaving in large numbers of 12oz rainbows is equally undesirable, especially where the natural food supply is so impoverished that there is no chance of these fish ever gaining weight. Trout do not feed on water! Some of the newer and more naïve fishery managers seem unaware of this startling fact.

Now a last word about fixed limits to the number of fish caught. This varies greatly, depending on many factors, between one brace and no limit whatever. While I personally deprecate some aspects of the way some stillwater fisheries are now run, I think that much can be said for the interesting day ticket system now operated at some others. Each angler pays a very small fee for the right to fish, and thereafter can catch as many fish as he pleases. These are then surrendered at the fishing hut, or may be purchased at so much per pound. A less extreme form of this strategy would be to charge a low entrance fee and then a compulsory fee of so much per pound of fish caught. When an angler could afford no more fish, he would have to stop fishing. This would avoid the frustration which many anglers encounter in embarking on a day's fishing and, by luck, catching their limit within the first hour. It also alleviates the fury of the angler who has paid a fat fee for his day's fishing and ends the day with nothing to show for it. Evidence strongly indicates that he is unlikely to return as a customer to that particular fishery.

One last point and I have done: it may come as a strange finale. At a time when even celebrated fisheries find it hard to make ends meet, why do not more rivers advertise and charge for autumn and winter grayling fishing? I am sure such publicity would lead many new anglers to try their hand at grayling fishing, and it would do something to enhance the profitability of the fisheries. As someone who has immensely enjoyed winter grayling fishing on a virtually free basis for many years, it never ceases to amaze me that such a saleable commodity should not be called upon to show a profit, even if a modest one. If that winter cash could be partly used to improve the summer trout water, we should all feel well satisfied.

Recommended Books for Further Reading

Trout Farming Handbook S. Drummond Sedgwick (2nd edition 1976) Seeley, Service & Co. Ltd., London.

An Angler's Entomology J. R. Harris (2nd edition 1956) Collins, London.

The Trout W. E. Frost and M. E. Brown (1970) Collins (Fontana), London.

The Pursuit of Stillwater Trout Brian Clarke (1975) Adam & Charles Black, London.

Grayling R. V. Righyni (1968) Macdonald, London.

Trout Flies of Stillwater John Goddard (4th edition 1979) Adam & Charles Black, London.

Trout Fly Recognition John Goddard (3rd edition 1976) Adam & Charles Black, London.

Small-River Fly Fishing for Trout and Grayling James Evans (1972) Adam & Charles Black, London.

Life in Lakes & Rivers T. T. Macan and E. B. Worthington (1974) Collins, London.

The Management of Angling Waters Alex Behrendt (1977) André Deutsch, London.

Fisherman's Fly David Jaques (1965) Adam & Charles Black, London.

Sea Trout Fishing Jock Scott (1969) Seeley, Service & Co. Ltd., London.

British Freshwater Fishes Margaret E. Varley (1967) Fishing News (Books) Ltd., London.

Studies on Loch Lomond P. S. Maitland (1966) University of Glasgow Press, Scotland.

Handbook of Trout and Salmon Diseases R. J. Roberts and C. J. Shepherd (1975) Fishing News (Books) Ltd., London.

The Trout E. Schwiebert (1979) André Deutsch, London.

The Complete Freshwater Fishes of the British Isles Jonathan Newdick (1979) Adam & Charles Black, London.

Index